Athletics in the United Kingdom

The rise and fall of the British Athletic Federation

by

John Lister

First published in the UK 2011
by Tatham Publishing

ISBN 978 0 9568105 0 2

Copyright © John Lister 2011

John Lister has asserted his right to be identified
as the author of this Work in accordance with the
Copyright Designs and Patents Act 1988.

All rights reserved. No part of this book may be
reproduced, stored in or introduced into a retrieval system,
or transmitted, in any form, or by any means (electronic,
mechanical, photocopying, recording or otherwise) without
the prior written permission of the publisher.

CONTENTS

Foreword · · · · · · Page 2

The Birth of BAF

Introduction	Page 4
The battle for BAF – the first steps	Page 9
The Turner Committee	Page 14
The baton is passed to the BAAB	Page 21
The Evans report	Page 25
The McAllister plan	Page 28
Courting the women; will they? won't they?	Page 33
Bring back Evans	Page 37
The home straight?	Page 42
England still not satisfied	Page 48
The ticking time bombs	Page 51
BAF is born	Page 55

The Business of Athletics

Introduction	Page 58
The Joint Standing Committee (JSC)	Page 62
The BAAB goes bust	Page 69
Management challenges	Page 76
A Chief Executive at last	Page 81
A poisoned chalice?	Page 86
Athletics and television	Page 97
The end of a beautiful friendship?	Page 103

Andy Norman · · · · · · Page 112

What about the athletes? · · · · · · Page 118

Epilogue · · · · · · Page 129

Where are they now? · · · · · · Page 134

Past Officers · · · · · · Page 138

FOREWORD

When I was elected as the Honorary Treasurer of the AAA in 1986, I did not anticipate that what would follow would be ten years of organisational upheaval that would leave lasting changes in the way that athletics in Britain is run.

When I finally relinquished my position in 1996, I had accumulated a mass of records, including virtually complete sets of all the minutes of the key meetings as well as voluminous correspondence, memoranda, press cuttings, etc. that covered the period. Taken together, all these papers represented a record of the process of administrative reform as well as of the management of the commercial business of the sport that kept the show on the road.

With the advent of UK Athletics following the demise of the British Athletic Federation, it gradually dawned on me that it might be important that these momentous changes should be written down and not left to moulder in old files. I decided to have a go, realising that, to a large extent, however impartial I tried to be, my own experiences and point of view would inevitably show through. Others involved at the time will have their own perspectives on the period and, indeed, my own part in it. I often felt that I was in the eye of a storm and readily acknowledge that many colleagues and others played different, but important, roles in steering athletics through a period that, in many ways, was an administrative failure but, simultaneously, achieved a consolidation of the sport that was necessary to modernise it and provide a firm foundation for the future.

At the same time that the management was wrestling with often controversial change, the athletes were going through a golden period of great success and a generation of superstars kept the British flag flying at the top of the mast.

I have tried to describe all these elements and apologise in advance for any errors or omissions, which are all my responsibility. I would also like to thank those who were kind enough to look at my drafts and to offer valuable suggestions for improvement.

Foreword

Most of my narrative is based on my personal experience as well as records but, after I relinquished the treasurership in 1996, I was not personally involved in any of the business of the BAF although, as the British representative on the European Athletic Association Council (I had been elected the year before) I continued to attend meetings of the BAF Council and received copies of management board minutes. The remainder of my narrative is, therefore, based not on personal experience but on these and other documents and conversations with some of those who continued to be involved.

Having now completed this task, I can finally dispose of all my files and I am very pleased that, upon the initiative of Tom McNab, Peter Radford, Jack Miller and others, the *Sports Archive Foundation* has been created so that they can find a new home.

I must also thank Mark Shearman for kindly providing most of the photographs.

John Lister/2011

THE BIRTH OF BAF

Introduction

On 14th August 1991, a lunch was held at the Randolph Hotel, Oxford to mark the end of the Amateur Athletic Association's traditional role in British athletics and to usher in a new, modern, era under the umbrella of the British Athletic Federation. The great and the good of athletics were present to enjoy a modest lunch (ratatouille terrine, fillet of salmon, chocolate torte and coffee) and, after the formal toast to The Queen had been proposed by Dr Bill Evans, chairman of the General Committee, Cliff Temple, the popular coach and athletics correspondent of the *Sunday Times*, rose to propose the toast to "The Association". After listening to Temple's words on the AAA's place in the history of the sport, Arthur McAllister, the President, responded by painting a picture of the future as he saw it.

The proceedings concluded with presentations to the officers of the AAA, Women's AAA and the Welsh AAA of mementoes and certificates of appreciation signed by HRH the Duke of Edinburgh, President of the BAAB, a ceremonial signing of the minutes of the last AAA General Committee meeting and the singing of Auld Lang Syne.

The choice of venue for the final lunch was significant as it was at the Randolph Hotel that the AAA had been formed 111 years before.

Organised sport had existed in Britain for more than 200 years but, in the late nineteenth century, with Queen Victoria still on the throne, it entered a new phase with the spread of *the governing body* as something more than an entity that merely created rules.

The Football Association was founded in 1863; the Rugby Football Association in 1871; and the Amateur Swimming Association in 1873.

In athletics, the Amateur Athletic Club appeared in 1866 but enjoyed only a short life, until 1880, when the Amateur Athletic Association (AAA) was formed.

The first edition of the Olympic Games of the modern era would not be staged until 16 years later, in 1896.

The Birth of BAF - Introduction

Although the Northern Counties Association had been established the year before, in 1879, the AAA was, if not the first, one of the first national governing bodies of athletics in the world and it set many of the basic rules of the sport that still apply today. In fact, many of the technical specifications such as the heights of hurdles and the weights of throwing implements were set in imperial measurements and simply converted to metric when athletics needed worldwide specifications. Thus, the internationally defined height of the men's high hurdle is 1.067m, equivalent to 3ft 6inches, and the weight of the men's shot is 7.26kg which is the nearest equivalent to the British 16lbs.

The AAA was established as the governing body of **men's** athletics in **England.** In 1948, the AAA reorganised itself as a limited company and agreed to a request from the Welsh men for the Welsh AAA to be included on the same footing as the existing area associations representing the North, Midlands and South of England, thereby becoming the governing body for England and Wales. Quite independently, equivalent bodies had been established in Scotland and Northern Ireland as well as for women and cross country so that, by the mid 20th century, athletics in the UK had a plethora of "governing bodies".

This was unsatisfactory to the International Amateur Athletic Federation (IAAF) which had been formed in 1913 as the governing body of world athletics and had initially recognised the AAA as Britain's international representative organisation. In 1931, the Scots made an application to affiliate directly to the IAAF but this was refused and, as a result, the British Amateur Athletic Board (BAAB) was formed in 1932 as a hybrid organisation to represent the then eight principal British governing bodies (AAA, Scotland, Wales and Northern Ireland; men and women separately in each case) as the UK member of the IAAF.

This arrangement continued for many years although, from time to time, there were calls for rationalisation.

The first serious attempt at modernisation was initiated at the 1960 AGM of the AAA when newly elected treasurer Phil Gale urged *"the immediate reorganisation of British athletics, with a United Kingdom AAA replacing the four governing bodies – the AAA, Scottish AAA, Northern Ireland AAA and Women's AAA"*. The proposal was carried but the other three bodies all emphatically stated that *"they were fully satisfied with the existing arrangement and would not support a change"*

The Birth of BAF - Introduction

A few years on the AAA was deeply in the red, the Annual Report for 1966/67 stating baldly that "*bankruptcy is a very real threat*". Against this background, a further attempt to rationalise the sport was made and resulted in the establishment of a committee, under the chairmanship of Lord Byers, a Liberal Peer, "*to examine the problems of the sport's development and to make recommendations*".

The Byers Committee reported in 1968 and, prior to its publication, the then Minister for Sport, Labour's Denis Howell, gave an interview to Tony Ward that was published in the *Sunday Times*. In a wide ranging discussion, Howell underlined the importance to Britain's reputation that athletics should be a successful sport but was critical of its administration. He said that he found the athletics structure "*baffling and complex and more professional administration is needed*".

The Byers committee had come to similar conclusions and reported in unequivocal terms –

"*We are of the opinion that the administration of British athletics needs a thorough overhaul. Firstly we find the case for one governing body for athletics in the UK to be proved beyond doubt and, secondly, we recommend that a new administrative organisation headed by a 'Director of British Athletics' be established.*"

Nothing happened.

In 1981, a new Minister for Sport, Conservative Neil Macfarlane, took office and was initially "*uncertain about the way in which athletics was organised*". He was, however, "*astonished to discover that there were no less than nineteen organisations (including, in those days, Tug-of-War) which had what must be regarded as a controlling interest in the sport*" and formed the opinion that "*with authority so fragmented, there was a danger that the best interests of athletics would be bypassed*".

He decided to set up an investigation, ostensibly into the finances of athletics, under the chairmanship of Dickie Jeeps, chairman of the Sports Council, and this was announced on 24 November 1982.

The AAA did not take kindly to the proposed investigation into its own affairs and felt that the committee should focus on the BAAB as the entity that effectively depended on Sports Council grants whereas the AAA did not. The AAA was also in the process of setting up its own committee to consider the establishment of one governing body for the UK and would

The Birth of BAF - Introduction

offer the Sports Council either representation or observer status there. It clearly felt that this would be going far enough.

Jeeps' committee, in its report, was critical of the way in which athletics lacked an organisational structure and recommended "*a unified and cohesive strategy for the development of the sport*". "*We can conclude*", said the committee, "*that the structure is not being used to make the best possible use of people and other resources or to provide a unity of purpose*".

Quite!

Around the same time, a new topic had arisen which directly touched the administration of the sport, not to mention its very ethos. Athletics was trying to come to terms with what was rapidly becoming the outdated concept of amateurism but which had been a cornerstone of the sport since Victorian times. Big money was starting to raise its head and "shamateurism" was rife. So, in its traditional way, the AAA had set up a committee to look into this. This committee, chaired by Dr Bill Evans, secretary of the Welsh AAA, had produced its report in September 1980 and recommended legitimising payments to athletes.

On 28th February 1981, the AAA had held an Extraordinary General Meeting (EGM) of its member clubs to discuss the Evans Report on amateurism and, somewhat surprisingly, the clubs present rejected it by a narrow margin (117 votes to 101).

Amongst the points made during the debate were that the AAA could not change the rules itself as the IAAF had jurisdiction; that it would be crazy if England and Wales but, perhaps, not Scotland accepted the new rules; and that, even if the rules were modernised in the ways proposed, the system of multiple governing bodies in the UK was in no state to manage and control the commercial forces that would be unleashed.

Ironically, the British Amateur Athletic Board had already been lobbying the IAAF to modernise the international rules concerning payments to athletes and had tabled a formal resolution with the IAAF to that effect. Despite the fact that the points made at the AAA EGM were valid, it was a considerable embarrassment to the BAAB that its most influential member had rejected the idea. The International Athletes' Club (IAC), which represented those most affected – the athletes - threatened to go to court to overturn the EGM decision but backed down after a promise by the AAA General Committee to look at the issue again.

The Birth of BAF - Introduction

There was much interest and discussion within the sport on the topic of payments to athletes and, following the EGM and some comments in *Athletics Weekly*, the British Athletic League (BAL - which comprised the country's leading clubs; and those to which most of the best athletes belonged) took a closer look at the topic and organised a meeting of persons who had shown a particular interest.

I had been involved in the BAL since its inception and was one of those who attended this meeting which was held on 11 April 1981 at the Post House hotel, Heathrow. The others who attended were Roger Simons (Shaftesbury Harriers), Derek Johnson (representing the International Athletes' Club), David Jeacock (Swindon AC), Neil Donachie (Edinburgh AC) and Jack Walters, chairman of the BAL. The deliberations of this group would eventually turn out to have a profound effect on the future direction of athletics in the UK.

The group's debate took an interesting turn. From a discussion about amateurism and the implications that athletes could become professional it became clear (at least to those present) that the existing unwieldy administrative structure of athletics would indeed struggle to manage the forces that could be released and that a new system was needed urgently – a single governing body; as recommended by Byers thirteen years before.

Soundings amongst the BAL member clubs indicated widespread support for both the concepts of moving towards "open" athletics and a single governing body for athletics in the UK. "Open athletics" would make no distinction between athletes who were paid for competing and those who were not and it should not be forgotten that, under the amateur rules then in force, any athletes accepting even small cash payments or value in kind could be barred from competing for life. With this encouragement, thus started a process that led to the creation of the British Athletic Federation which was formally approved 10 years later, almost to the day, on 17 March 1991.

But there would be many twists and turns, false dawns and false starts between 1981 and 1991 and the British Athletic Federation, created in controversy and conflict, would never achieve a peaceful existence before, itself, collapsing into administration in 1997 after a mere 6 years of life.

This account is an attempt to describe what happened.

THE BATTLE FOR BAF – THE FIRST STEPS

The British Athletic League (BAL) had emerged as the flag carrier for reform but, in order to achieve its objectives, publicity and a wider support base were needed. It was also essential to demonstrate that its arguments were credible and did, indeed, command support within the club structure of the sport. Further research was needed and, in order to test opinion and to produce clear recommendations, the BAL conducted a survey of its member clubs.

In February 1982, the BAL published the findings of its study and these included specific proposals for the creation of a single governing body. This report was circulated to all BAL clubs, to the AAA, the BAAB and their constituent associations and was also published in full in the 1 May 1982 issue of *Athletics Weekly*.

After rehearsing the case for a single governing body, the BAL proposed a structure based on the existing regional associations (Scotland, Wales, Northern Ireland, North of England, Midlands and South of England) overseen by a UK Association. For practical reasons (mainly its already well developed corporate constitution) the BAL recommended that the AAA be converted into the new UK AAA (the word Amateur would be dropped when athletics became open) and that the BAAB be disbanded. Clubs would be full voting members of their regional associations and of the UK AAA and there would be no separate body for England as such. At all levels, separate men's and women's organisations should merge.

Running magazine described the BAL report as *"the best argued and most constructive contribution to the debate in recent times"*.

In its March 1982 issue, *Running* magazine had published a three page article by leading athletics journalist Neil Wilson headed **who runs running?** a title that said it all. Wilson analysed the labyrinthine organisation of athletics in the UK and concluded that *"if they did not get up to date, they would deserve their fate"*.

Encouraged by the positive responses to its proposals, the BAL decided to organise an open meeting on the topic. This was held on 16 May 1982, again at the Post House hotel, Heathrow, and was chaired by former British athletic team captain Menzies Campbell, QC (subsequently to become an MP and leader of the Liberal Democratic Party). This open meeting took the debate a little further but revealed the need for a more organised campaign.

Accordingly, Roger Simons, on behalf of his British League club, Shaftesbury Harriers, submitted a motion to the Southern Counties AAA (a constituent part of the AAA) that there should be a single UK governing body. This was the first tentative step into the constitutional corridors of power but the proposal was ruled out of order on technical grounds at the body's June 1982 AGM. However, an informal vote at the same meeting showed a large majority in favour of the Shaftesbury-BAL proposal.

The 1982 summer season generated much press comment about the need to rationalise the amateur-professional status of athletes and, finally, at its Congress in Athens prior to the European Championships, the IAAF approved a proposal (presented by Britain's Andy Norman) that athletes' earnings would be legitimised provided that the monies were held in trust funds until they retired from the sport. The sport was moving on and John Rodda, athletics correspondent of the *Guardian* newspaper, wrote that "*It is more urgent than ever to have one controlling body in Britain*".

Despite the setback at the Southern Counties AGM, it was obvious that real progress could be made only by harnessing the formal constitutional procedures of the sport, particularly those of the AAA which was the most influential of the governing bodies. Indeed, the AAA was, in practice, even more powerful than the BAAB as it not only had a virtually inbuilt voting majority there but also organised, in competition with the BAAB, increasingly profitable televised events. There was certainly tension (bordering on open warfare) between the AAA and the BAAB which did not augur well for a co-operative approach of the countries of the UK to form themselves into a single entity but the proponents had no choice but to start with the most influential body, the AAA, as it was here, unlike the BAAB, that the clubs could vote.

Accordingly, a formal motion was presented to the AAA to be placed on the agenda of the 1982 AGM to be held in London on 6th November 1982. I formally proposed the motion on behalf of my club (Cardiff AAC) and it was seconded by Roger Simons on behalf of Shaftesbury Harriers. It was essential to comply strictly with the technical requirements of the AAA's constitution and in this Roger and I were greatly assisted by the expertise of solicitor David Jeacock.

The battle for BAF – the first steps

The motion contained four separate proposals:

1. It is the wish of this Association that Athletics in the United Kingdom be administered by a single governing body.

2. That this Association establishes a Working Party to seek ways and means of achieving the objective stated in Motion No. 1.

3. That the Working Party be composed of seven members appointed at this AGM (four of whom should not presently be members of any Committee of the Association) which seven members shall elect a chairman.

4. That the Working Party report back with recommendations to an Extraordinary General Meeting of the Association to be held not later than 30 April 1983.

The wording was amended by the AAA to:

1. That Athletics in the United Kingdom be administered by a single governing body.

2. That this Association establishes a Working Party to seek ways and means of achieving the objective stated in Motion No. 1.

3. That the Working Party report back with recommendations to a General Meeting of the Association.

At a well attended meeting, the motions were passed by overwhelming majorities; on a show of hands, only 4 were raised against the motions compared with some 200 in favour. The depth of feeling was demonstrated by the supportive proxy votes that had been submitted by those unable to attend the meeting in person. More than 600 such votes had been registered with the AAA, representing some 40% of the theoretical total voting strength of all the member clubs. This represented a resounding victory for club power but was to be only the first step on a long and difficult journey.

After the declaration of the vote, Arthur McAllister, the chairman of the General Committee, candidly acknowledged that the association (AAA), through its historical attitude to other associations, "*had a lot to answer for over the question of the Women's AAA. The association must be honest and admit that they had not given the women a fair crack of the whip and*

The battle for BAF – the first steps

would have to work hard if they wished them to become part of a new body."

The public reaction to the result of the meeting was overwhelmingly favourable with much positive press comment. A sour note was introduced by Ewan Murray, secretary of the Scottish AAA, who, in a typically withering comment, said that *"the Scots would not sell their sovereignty in any deal"* and *"I assume that we will hear from the AAA about their meeting on Saturday and be invited to take part in the working party"*.

The AGM vote could not be ignored by the AAA General Committee which duly appointed the required working party and invited Dr Mike Turner to be its chairman.

There was no place, however, for a Scottish representative nor, for that matter, any representative of any of the other governing bodies that would potentially be affected. Interestingly, the Women's AAA, which had spurned all previous overtures of possible amalgamation with the AAA, made no public comment. Perhaps wily, long serving honorary secretary Marea Hartman could sense which way the wind was blowing.

As Turner's working party started its deliberations, the campaigners set their sights on the Women's AAA, expected to be a hard nut to crack.

Back in 1975, an attempt had been made by Folkestone AC (where journalist Cliff Temple was the driving force) to get the AGM of the Women's AAA to consider the merits of amalgamation with the AAA. As we have also seen happen elsewhere, the motion was ruled out of order on a technicality but was, nevertheless, debated. Most of the speakers were aghast at the thought of a *"takeover by the men"* (one delegate, to great applause, asked why the women could not take over the men!) and there was great hilarity at the supposedly ludicrous suggestion that *"national championships for men and women could be staged together"*. Needless to say, the suggestion of amalgamation was roundly rejected.

The 1983 AGM of the Women's AAA was scheduled for 12th March. This time it was Swindon AC (led by solicitor David Jeacock along with club secretary Mary Wall) that submitted identical motions to those passed so successfully at the AGM of the AAA only four months before.

Proxy votes were not permitted at Women's AAA meetings and, on a show of hands, the motions were defeated by 50 votes to 41, whereupon Swindon demanded an Extraordinary General Meeting to consider the

The battle for BAF – the first steps

matter again. This was held on 23 April and decided that there should be a postal ballot of all the Association's member clubs on the original motions. The postal votes were in favour, with the upshot that, on 8 November 1983, the Women's AAA established a working party "*to seek ways and means of establishing a single governing body for athletics in the UK*".

At last, it appeared that the AAA and the Women's AAA might both be working in the same direction.

We shall see.

THE TURNER COMMITTEE

On 6th November 1982, the General Committee of the AAA had appointed the members of the committee *"to find ways and means of implementing the [1982 AGM] resolution that athletics in the United Kingdom be administered by a single governing body"*.

In typical fashion the committee was composed of representatives of the constituent area associations of the AAA plus others and a chairman.

The chairman, Mike Turner, was a don at Cambridge University, lecturing on land economy. He had been a good international athlete, representing England at cross country on many occasions, and had also served on a number of AAA or BAAB committees or working groups. He brought a calm and quiet efficiency to the role and did a good job.

Representing the Southern Counties AAA was Bill Lucas, a retired insurance broker and World War II RAF veteran. Charles Rice had run the Northern Counties AA as Honorary Secretary since 1969 and David Cropper, a Civil Engineer specialising in highway construction and former Olympic level 800m runner, had been Honorary Treasurer of the Midland Counties AAA since 1975. The Welsh AAA was represented by Reg Snow, a civil servant, who was a former Welsh international sprinter and Welsh team manager.

David Moorcroft, years later to be the first Chief Executive of UK Athletics, was a popular and distinguished international and Olympic athlete and the current holder of the 5,000m world record. Completing the committee were Roger and I (as we had led the campaign which had resulted in the setting up of the committee) and David Shaw, previously the General Secretary of the BAAB but who had resigned in frustration and was then working in television as the General Secretary of the ITV Association. Roger Simons was a construction industry manager and President of Shaftesbury Harriers and I was chairman of Cardiff AAC and a former Welsh International athlete; and, by profession, a chartered accountant.

The Turner Committee

Barry Willis, a respected former Honorary Secretary of the AAA, agreed to act as secretary to the committee.

The committee did not waste any time in getting down to its task and held its first meeting in London on 19 December 1982. The first bit of good news was that, at its AGM the previous day, the Scottish AAA had agreed to have an open mind towards the deliberations of the AAA's committee; a crack appearing rather than a breakthrough.

From the outset, the committee was conscious of the need to tread carefully, to consult widely and not to alienate bodies and individuals in athletics who were jealous of their independence and suspicious of what the AAA was up to. Many saw it as an attempted take-over.

The first tasks, therefore, were to analyse the existing situation and to set in train a process of consultation. These were to include face to face meetings with all existing governing bodies, a questionnaire, and an open letter to the principle athletics magazine, *Athletics Weekly*, inviting suggestions. It was important not to leave anybody out, even by accident.

In order to manage this process of consultation effectively, the committee divided itself up to share the burden. As at least nineteen separate organisations had been identified, all of whom could claim to have a role in the administration of athletics in the UK, not to mention other entities such as the Sport Councils and the IAAF, the challenge was considerable.

The committee worked extraordinarily hard with meetings at least monthly and visits to and meetings with other bodies in addition. In fact, the committee met formally fifteen times in the ten months prior to its final meeting on 23 October 1983.

Numerous nettles needed to be grasped, none more ticklish than the odd positions of the Welsh AAA and the Welsh Women's AAA. Representing a nation within the United Kingdom, as opposed to an area of England, these two associations were full members of the BAAB alongside the AAA, the Women's AAA, Scottish men and women and Northern Irish men and women. HOWEVER, the Welsh AAA was also an area association member of the AAA and this was thought to be unfair as it gave the Welsh AAA two bites at the cherry. But it was worse, as the Welsh AAA sometimes voted against the views of the AAA (regarded as its parent body) in meetings of the BAAB. The Welsh women had taken a different

The Turner Committee

line by seceding from a position within the Women's AAA some years before.

One of the more interesting, and illuminating, of the consultations was that with the IAAF as here was a chance to discover how athletics in Britain was seen from outside. The then General Secretary of the IAAF, John Holt, had taken the trouble to prepare a discussion paper in advance of the meeting.

The paper underlined that Great Britain was seen as a very important athletic nation but that *"The greatest difficulty facing the BAAB is one of identity. IAAF members are confused at the roles of the BAAB, AAA, SAAA (Scotland), separate organisations for cross country, road running, and race walking and the various women's equivalents."*

As I have already mentioned, an important issue facing the IAAF at the time was the advent of official money payments to athletes and how to manage them. A system of athletes' trust funds was being introduced but, *"we await details of the British system; however it is apparent that the fact that multiple associations exist has created a difficulty....."*.

The meetings with the existing 19 (and more) UK organisations, however, left the clear impression that they did not see the confusion described by the IAAF and, by and large, felt that the present system did not need fundamental change although conceding (who wouldn't?) that there could be improvements.

The attitude of the BAAB itself was more positive. Chairman Bill Evans (who was to play a leading role in the eventual formation of the British Athletic Federation) stated quite clearly that he favoured the single governing body being worked out by the Turner Committee although, revealingly, rather assumed that it would be *"an extension of the BAAB"*.

It was, of course, essential that the committee met the officers of the AAA itself. The Chairman, Arthur McAllister, Treasurer John Martell and General Secretary Mike Farrell took pains to stress that they were expressing their personal views only, which seemed rather at odds with the reason for consulting them. Indeed, bearing in mind the strength of feeling expressed by the member clubs at the fateful 1982 AGM, Mike Farrell, in a letter to Mike Turner commenting on the notes of the meeting, concluded preposterously by saying that *"John Martell, Arthur McAllister and myself feel that we should be looking to the working party to convince us and the AAA that a UK body is wholly needed, and this has not yet been*

The Turner Committee

demonstrated to us...". Had they forgotten that the remit of the committee, carefully drafted by McAllister's own General Committee, was *"to seek ways to **implement** the resolution that Athletics in the United Kingdom be administered by a single governing body"?* The Turner committee was working on the assumption that the merits of the argument had already been accepted. But, then, McAllister, Martell and Farrell were expressing only their personal views, weren't they?

The final report of the committee was signed off in November 1983 and made 13 principal recommendations of which the five key ones were:

No.1.   That a United Kingdom Amateur Athletic Association (UKAAA) shall be formed as "the only national governing body for all amateur athletics" in the United Kingdom of Great Britain and Northern Ireland.

No.2.   That the UKAAA shall be formed by means of an agreement by the Member Associations of the BAAB, to dissolve the BAAB and to transfer the right of affiliation to the IAAF from the Board to the UKAAA.

No.9.   That the AAA shall amend its constitution so as to redefine its area of responsibility as extending exclusively to England.

No.10. That the Welsh AAA shall become independent of the AAA and wholly responsible for all matters affecting the administration of athletics in Wales.

No.13. That the men's and women's Associations in each of the four home countries shall be encouraged to amalgamate.

There had been some discussion about what to call the new body and it was decided to opt for *United Kingdom AAA*, recognising the historical significance of the three letters *AAA* and also to be consistent with the names of the constituent home countries and regions.

The report itself discussed the potential benefits that would flow from a streamlining of the sport, the conclusions of the consultation process, the structure of the new body that it recommended and the possible ways in which the new body could be created.

A limited liability company was proposed, with all clubs of the UK having voting powers at General Meetings. The managing council would be based on representation from the four home countries (England, Scotland, Wales and Northern Ireland) plus the chairmen of various standing committees (Coaching, International, Development and so on) and certain of the professional staff. There should be an executive of the senior professional directors under a chief executive.

The new roles of the national associations were discussed as were the possible terms on which a secession of the Welsh AAA from the AAA could be negotiated. Special interest groups such as cross country, leagues, international athletes, and others, including the role of women, were all addressed. The financial implications and potential opportunities were laid out at length.

Three possible ways of setting up the new body were considered. Firstly, the AAA could expand itself to embrace the rest of the UK under a new name and corporate constitution. This had been suggested by the BAL and offered some potential benefit as the AAA was already incorporated as a limited liability company, but was rejected as having too much of the flavour of an AAA take-over.

Alternatively, the BAAB could be turned into a limited company with a drastically revised constitution and there was some merit in this as the BAAB was the existing member of the IAAF. However, despite the important role that it played, the BAAB was criticised for being undemocratic and out of touch (clubs could attend AGMs but not vote and David Bedford had memorably, even though perhaps unfairly, described the organisation as *"a Sunday afternoon's women's knitting society"*) and it was decided that the best plan would be to create an entirely new entity. The BAAB would be wound up and the AAA would restrict itself exclusively to England (and, hopefully, merge with the Women's AAA).

The report was formally presented by Mike Turner and Barry Willis to the influential Finance and General Purposes Committee of the AAA on 26 November 1983; which was too late for its inclusion in the business of the 1983 Annual General Meeting, which had been the target date. This was actually no bad thing as, instead, the report could be the centre of attention at a specially convened General Meeting (EGM) and not submerged in the general business of an AGM.

The Turner Committee

It had been expected that the AAA would not lose any time in calling an EGM to debate the report but, by January 1984, no progress was evident and the campaigners, frustrated, decided to requisition one, as they were entitled to do if they could get the support of 10 per cent of the voting membership of the AAA. Although reluctant to try the patience of club secretaries again, it was felt that there was no option as, otherwise, the AAA would probably delay the whole matter until the 1984 AGM, an unacceptably long time off.

So the process of canvassing support started once again and, under pressure, the AAA set a date, 9th June 1984, for the important EGM. But there was a twist.

Despite the existence of a valid requisition from clubs, the AAA's General Committee seized the initiative by itself calling the EGM and thereby gaining control of the wording of the motions to be considered. The wording of the AAA's primary motion was:

> That the Amateur Athletic Association through its General Committee promotes and supports the formation of a new athletic body as "the only National Governing Body for all Amateur Athletics in the United Kingdom of Great Britain and Northern Ireland" by the expansion of the constitution and activities of the B.A.A.B to embrace all matters affecting the administration of athletics in the United Kingdom.

Whereas this, taken together with subsidiary motions, supported, in general, the proposals of the Turner Committee, there were significant differences. The proposal from the AAA's General Committee (under the chairmanship of Arthur McAllister, of whom much more, later) was that the single governing body should be a reconstituted BAAB (Turner had recommended an entirely new entity) and that the area associations of the AAA should be included in the managing council (Turner had recommended the four home countries only).

This annoyed the campaigners who also saw it as a rearguard action by the diehards who simply did not want any fundamental change. In fact, at the EGM itself, David Bedford baldly stated that "*a vote for the General Committee would be a vote for no change*".

The outcome, following negotiations with the officers of the AAA, was that the original proposals from the AAA, amended slightly, would be tabled along with an amendment in the name of Cardiff AAC that the Turner alternative be accepted. Thus, the EGM could choose and the lobbying started once again.

The EGM, which included a presentation of the report by Mike Turner, lasted four hours and, at the end, the amendment (to adopt the Turner approach) was defeated by the narrow margin of 214 votes to 184. The AAA's proposal was then accepted unanimously. Unfortunately, a postal strike had resulted in approximately 150 proxy votes arriving late and not being counted; who knows whether these would have affected the result?

This result represented a setback for the campaigners but at least the principle of a single governing body was now firmly established as a mandated objective of the AAA.

THE BATON IS PASSED TO THE BAAB

After getting its way at the June 1984 EGM, the AAA was now finally faced with having to do something about this hot potato so it decided to pass it to the BAAB. The EGM resolution, carefully crafted by the AAA, had recommended that the BAAB be re-vamped into a single governing body so who better than the BAAB to see if it could be done?

In January 1985, in response to the AAA, the BAAB, as expected, agreed to "*set up a steering committee to look at ways and means of establishing a new athletic body as the only National Governing Body for all amateur athletics in the United Kingdom... by the expansion of the constitution and the activities of the BAAB to embrace all matters affecting the administration of athletics in the UK*".

Dr Bill Evans, a former chairman of the BAAB and the current Honorary Secretary of the Welsh AAA, was appointed as chairman and he and his new committee got down to work.

As a precursor to these moves the AAA had taken steps to have itself granted additional votes on the BAAB so that it was in a stronger position than ever to influence its decisions. It had also proposed Mike Turner as the Honorary Treasurer of the BAAB and he had been duly elected at the 1984 AGM.

At the AGM of the BAAB held on 25 November 1984 voting rights had been changed so that, at General Meetings, the AAA wielded 90 votes out of a total of 220. The Women's AAA would have 30 votes so that, with 120 votes between them, the English had an inbuilt majority. As a protection against abuse, it was decided that changes to the constitution would need 150 votes but this needed only one of the Celtic countries to side with England.

The slightly farcical arrangement of the BAAB was that essentially the same people comprised the managing Council as were entitled to vote at General Meetings. The Council included one representative each of the male and female international athletes but, otherwise, the Council members' votes were allocated in identical proportions to those at General Meetings. This meant that, from time to time, General Meetings of the BAAB had to be organised so that the members could ratify decisions that they themselves had already made, but as members of the Council.

As we have seen, clubs were entitled to attend and speak at General Meetings of the BAAB but had no votes.

It was no wonder that the BAAB was not held in high regard.

The Evans committee proceeded at a snail's pace. At the 1985 AGM of the AAA, Bill Evans was able to say only that "*he was not discouraged but it was not an easy task to persuade some people to become more flexible in their approach*". But, "*he believed that one governing body would come about because of the athletic clubs' support for the idea*". Astonishingly, the minutes of the 1985 AGM of the BAAB itself, held three weeks later, did not even mention the subject. To be fair to Bill Evans, he was always a believer in the concept and strove valiantly and ultimately successfully to see the dream achieved.

No doubt sensing which way the Evans wind was blowing, the International Athletes' Club (IAC) entered the debate in February 1986 and suggested the setting up of an entirely new UK governing body with a "club-based constitution". This had been drafted by Derek Johnson and, in an indication of battles to come, argued for direct representation on the body's executive board from the area associations of England.

The year 1985 had, however, marked a turning point for athletics in Britain in a different way. The finances of the sport were transformed by lucrative new television and marketing agreements that saw income soar but, as will be seen, this bonanza placed even more strain on the fragmented administration of the sport and underlined the need for strong central management more than ever.

A further year passed and, to the amazement of many, the Annual Report of the AAA for 1986 contained not a single word about the one governing body project; except for an addendum slip added at the last minute which said, without comment, that the Evans Committee "*had produced a report that could be obtained from the AAA on request*".

There was one item on the agenda of that AGM, however, that might turn out to influence matters; the election of a new Honorary Treasurer.

The Southern Counties AAA had long been one of the more entrepreneurial and politically active of the Area Associations of the AAA and, amongst its supporters, former athletic stars David Bedford and Derek Johnson were flexing their muscles. David and Derek effectively ran the

The baton is passed to the BAAB

International Athletes Club (IAC) between them, an organisation representing arguably the most important element of the sport (the international athletes) and which promoted a popular and lucrative Grand Prix spectacular each year at Crystal Palace stadium.

The sport's activists were becoming frustrated with, as they saw them, the anachronistic ways of the AAA and sought an opportunity to gain some greater influence on the inside.

In an attempt to open up its management, Derek Johnson, on behalf of the IAC, had proposed at the 1985 AGM of the AAA the direct election of club representatives to the General Committee. This received a majority of votes but not enough to satisfy the 75% threshold needed for it to be enacted. A different approach was needed.

Midlander David Cropper had become the Honorary Treasurer of the AAA at the 1985 AGM following the retirement of John Martell and was struggling to find enough time. Additionally, British athletics had struck TV gold through a huge increase in rights fees offered by ITV in its successful bid to oust the BBC from its previously unchallenged position as the broadcaster of athletics in Britain. TV and marketing revenue had shot up as a result and this needed managing. I had been involved in the one governing body campaign from the outset and, with my professional qualifications, the Southern Counties felt that I would be a good choice for the treasurer's position and, to my surprise but with my agreement, proposed me in place of Cropper who had decided he could not give enough time.

The proposal apparently did not go down very well with some within the AAA hierarchy and General Committee chairman Arthur McAllister attempted to persuade Roger Simons to stand for the position instead. Simons honourably refused as a matter of principle as he had supported my nomination within the Southern Counties and thus, as the sole candidate, I was elected Honorary Treasurer of the AAA at the AGM on 6th December 1986.

I had been totally surprised to be approached, out of the blue, by the Southern Counties and saw the possibility of occupying one of the most senior positions in the sport as a great honour. I also realised that, as one of the protagonists for the one governing body, I would be in a position on the inside to push. Furthermore, as an officer of the AAA, I would automatically be a member of the Council of the BAAB and could take a personal interest in the machinations of the Evans committee.

The baton is passed to the BAAB

My election as Honorary Treasurer brought together in key positions in the sport two who had known each other and worked together for years. Bill Evans and I were Welsh, we both lived in Cardiff and were both long standing members and officials of the same athletic club, Cardiff AAC.

Bill Evans was a university academic, head of the Zoology Department at the University of Wales, Cardiff, and something of an expert on exotic insects. He had got involved in athletics when his son, a good sprinter, joined Cardiff AAC and he, together with his wife Kath, became more and more involved in the administration of the club, where they were both highly regarded. After stints as Secretary and Chairman of his club, Bill Evans moved on to become a long serving Honorary Secretary of the Welsh AAA. This position gave him an automatic place on the General Committee of the AAA where he quickly made his mark as a quietly efficient administrator. As Honorary Secretary of the Welsh association, he also had an automatic place on the Council of the BAAB and progressed to be its chairman for four years from 1980 to 1984.

I had competed as an athlete for Wales over a long period and had been one of a group of like minded athletes who, in the late 1960s, had pushed through the amalgamation of two Cardiff clubs to form Cardiff AAC, a club that was to dominate British club athletics for a number of years. I had also been involved in the formation and early development of the British Athletic League and, having had an interest in the administrative side of athletics from an early age, had been treasurer of the Cardiff club since 1968 as well as taking on the chair for a second time in 1981. I was well aware that my sudden elevation directly from a club base to one of the most responsible positions in the sport in Britain was, to say the least, unusual and caused a few raised eyebrows.

Having been elected Honorary Treasurer on the Saturday, I made my first visit to the London offices of the AAA the following Monday for an introductory tour by General Secretary Mike Farrell and left rather shocked by what I encountered – but more of that later.

THE EVANS REPORT

On 11 October 1986, Bill Evans presented his committee's report to the BAAB Council which decided to discuss it early in the New Year, two years after it had appointed the Evans Committee.

In a rather woolly report, the committee had delved into a lot of detail but fudged some key issues. It identified *possible* member associations of the new body, which did not include clubs, but then went on to say that clubs would be *invited* to the AGM with votes and it even proposed detailed voting rights according to size. It proposed a Council that would meet only twice a year with a membership based on nations, not regions, plus special interest groups such as cross country, veterans, international athletes and schools. Day to day management would be in the hands of a Management Board. A chief executive was considered but rejected in favour of a part time chairman of the management board who would receive an honorarium (£5,000 p.a. was suggested). No attempt was made to address the financial consequences of the reorganisation and the special position of the AAA was not mentioned. However, it had proposed a name – British Athletic Federation (BAF).

The flame seemed to be barely flickering if not quite out.

At its meeting on 14th February 1987, the BAAB Council decided to move the matter on by commissioning a draft of a Constitution and a financial plan. The General Secretary of the BAAB (Nigel Cooper) was tasked with producing a draft constitution and the responsibility for the financial plan was given to the finance committee – in practice to the treasurer of the BAAB (Mike Turner, he of the Turner report) and to me, as treasurer of the AAA.

As a harbinger of things to come, the Southern Counties AAA circulated their observations on the report. Whilst generally supportive, the South wanted direct representation from the three English area associations to the managing council, not indirectly through the English AAA as suggested by Evans. They also criticised the lack of funding proposals and said that the BAF must be provided with sufficient start up capital to ensure its viability.

By the end of May 1987, Nigel Cooper and Bill Evans had produced a draft constitution and Mike Turner and I had produced a financial appraisal based on the draft constitution. It was intended that these would come together and be put before the BAAB Council, hopefully for approval, on 7th July.

But then disaster struck; as I shall describe in more detail later, the BAAB was in financial trouble, which meant that everything else was shelved for the time being. The financial position was revealed to be so serious that the BAAB came close to being wound up there and then but the AAA, not for the first time, was called upon to bail out the BAAB; but exacted conditions.

In return for guaranteeing the BAAB's debts, the AAA demanded that it take over the direct management of the BAAB's affairs (under what was to be called the "caretakership") and, furthermore, needed additional voting power to enforce its will.

In the face of this financial reality, the BAAB accepted the AAA's "offer" and, at a special Extraordinary General Meeting on 10th October 1987, granted the AAA an additional six votes at Council meetings. This gave the AAA 15 votes out of a total of 30, not an outright majority, which was thought to be too brutal, but enough to get its way.

Along with the financial deal, the AAA extracted an agreement that a deadline of 1 January 1989 (some 15 months hence) would be set for the establishment of the one governing body. There was some discussion about how this was to be achieved and it was eventually agreed that, as the AAA was now in charge, the responsibility should be passed back to them.

The AAA President, Arthur McAllister, agreed to lead the project forward and to produce the necessary constitution. He was very conscious of the need for speed as the vital TV and marketing contracts would run out in March 1990 and negotiations for their renewal would be starting in early 1989. Indeed, Andy Norman had made this point very forcibly during the debate and TV executives had been looking for reassurances that they would have a credible organisation to deal with.

Somewhat boldly, as it turned out, McAllister said that *"I am not going to have a working group that produces another report, like Byers, Turner, Evans and others: we've got to get on quickly with constructing the new body, to maintain the confidence of the sponsors and television with whom we will be in negotiation within 18 months. I would hope to have a new constitution drawn up by March next year [1988] but I hope no one is going to hold us to that.*

We are going to move swiftly; we will make mistakes but hopefully they will not be big ones."

Brave words indeed.

THE McALLISTER PLAN

Arthur McAllister, a died in the wool Yorkshire man, had held many of the senior positions in British athletics and had been chairman of the AAA's General Committee until 1986 when he stepped up to become President, handing over the chairmanship to Midlander Bill Ferguson.

In his younger days, McAllister had been a competent and effective administrator but, later, became more and more focused on his Northern, and especially, English roots. By profession he had spent most of his life teaching individuals with what are now called special needs; Arthur, as everybody, would have called them handicapped. With his background, he probably felt uncomfortable as athletics evolved more commercially and was on the brink of becoming an openly professional sport as this would have clashed with his amateur instincts. This led to occasional  flashes of temper when, with a barely concealed sneer, he would refer to some of his colleagues as "*only businessmen*", implying, unfairly, that they were only interested in the money in sport and not the sport itself. Nevertheless, Arthur McAllister was generally liked and respected for what he had done for his sport and undoubtedly worked sincerely and hard to achieve what he saw as the best outcome.

Having been asked by the BAAB to do so, Arthur McAllister did indeed produce his draft BAF constitution as promised. This was presented to the respective meetings of the AAA and BAAB in May 1988 and whereas the BAAB rather docilely largely went along the proposals (not surprising, considering the number of votes held by the AAA), there was trouble brewing within the AAA itself.

A split had opened up over the composition of the managing council where McAllister (as Evans and Turner before) had proposed a seat for the (yet to be established) purely English Association, with nine representatives. His first draft gave these 9 representatives two votes each but this was watered down in the final proposal so that these nine would wield 15 votes, more than all the others combined. This would have given the English absolute control and, of itself, would be controversial enough,

The McAllister Plan

but the Southern Counties AAA objected even to the basic concept of a seat exclusively for England and preferred that each of the three English regions should be directly represented instead.

A fire had been lit and was to burn brightly.

McAllister persevered with his plan and obtained the support of the AAA General Committee (with the Southern Counties representatives abstaining) to put them to an EGM of the AAA to be specially convened for the purpose on 3rd July 1988.

The Southern Counties AAA was by now taking a more aggressive part in the debate and produced its own "six principles" that the BAF should be based upon. The essential difference from McAllister was that the managing council would include direct representation from the three English area associations and that the English should not have an automatic inbuilt majority.

Derek Johnson had by now emerged as the loudest voice from the Southern Counties and had been the principal author of the "six principles". What his ultimate motive might be was not clear but, at a AAA Finance & General Purposes Committee meeting prior to the EGM, he claimed that the South "*were fighting for their life*" and "*did not intend to allow themselves to be continually intimidated by their colleagues from the other areas*".

Derek Johnson had won a silver medal in the 800m at the Olympic Games of 1956 in a race which has been described as "one of the most thrilling in Olympic annals". He had studied at Oxford University and was set on a medical career until illness intervened. An articulate and intelligent man, he pursued a business career and gradually established a base (not to mention an income) in athletics through the International Athletes' Club where he played an important role in establishing and organising, in partnership with the younger David Bedford, an annual televised athletic spectacular at Crystal Palace stadium. His friendship with David  Bedford grew and together they made a move into the politics of athletics through the Southern Counties AAA.

The McAllister Plan

In 1987, Derek Johnson became Assistant Treasurer of the Southern Counties and persuaded its General Committee that he should have "*special responsibility for the South's financial relationship with the AAA*". In what could be seen as a sign of trouble ahead, he wrote to the Treasurer Martin Cartwright that he, Johnson, should replace Cartwright on the powerful AAA's Finance and General Purposes Committee, with the scarcely veiled threat that, otherwise, he would challenge Cartwright for his position. Cartwright declined and, within a year, Johnson was the Treasurer of the Southern Counties AAA (with Cartwright his assistant) and was to use his position to become a thorn in the flesh of the AAA.

At the same time, David Bedford became the Assistant Honorary Secretary of the Southern Counties and the stage was set for what was to come.

Despite considerable efforts by McAllister and others behind the scenes to find common ground on the draft constitution, it proved impossible to bridge the gap between the alternative views and the EGM was duly convened. The clubs would have to decide between the McAllister proposals and an amendment from the Southern Counties that their six principles should prevail.

The scene was set for a showdown; and so it proved.

The battle became dirty with, seemingly, much at stake.

First out of the blocks was the AAA with a press release called **Federation News**. The first line of this betrayed its credibility by stating that "*the clubs of **England** will meet to decide the sort of Federation (BAF) they envisage*" Had Wales (still part of the AAA) been airbrushed out?

The South hit back with "**THE HIDDEN AGENDA**", claiming that the McAllister plan would effectively disfranchise the clubs.

The Women's AAA weighed in on the side of McAllister; and why wouldn't they as England, with men and women combined, would rule the roost?

And so it went on, with much outpouring of ink and money on increasingly vitriolic advertisements in *Athletics Weekly* and circulars to clubs, until the shoot-out had to be finally settled by voting.

The McAllister Plan

Writing in the *Sunday Times*, Cliff Temple observed that *"The hyperactive Southern Counties AAA, urged on by the former Olympic athletes Dave Bedford and Derek Johnson, are strongly opposing McAllister's plan because they contend it will remove so much influence from the regions."*

Temple went on to say that, *"Sadly, the whole issue has been turned by the South, led by Bedford and Johnson, into the same type of direct confrontation which they have been staging for years with the existing administration because of their involvement with the International Athletes' Club."*

Because of the level of animosity and public comment that had been generated, McAllister, fearing a technical slip up, even felt it necessary to get written legal advice on the procedures and conduct of the meeting. Usually the President (McAllister) would chair an EGM but as he was the author of the proposals to be voted on, the chairman of the General Committee, Bill Ferguson, was to chair the meeting in his place.

McAllister made the case for his plan and I, as the treasurer, was called upon to second the proposal.

I had found myself in rather a dilemma as, in fact, the Southern proposals were akin to those that I had drafted and which had been agreed by the British Athletic League what seemed light years before. My overriding worry, as Treasurer, however, was that, if the issue was not settled quickly, the chances of new TV and marketing contracts would diminish if not disappear. The idea of English control was also seductive as, from a practical point of view, it would effectively continue the AAA's "caretakership" that, by now, was starting to turn around the commercial and financial fortunes of the sport. Although sympathetic to them from a democratic point of view, I feared that the "six principles" might lead to a return to the old fragmented mismanagement that had got the AAA and BAAB into financial trouble.

Ironically, I ended up on the opposite side of the debate to Roger Simons who was the formal proposer of the Southern amendment. We had both served on the Turner Committee that had opted for English, not area, representation but time had moved on, as had the politics. Derek Johnson, in his contribution, argued for the new federation to be formed by an expansion of the AAA; the original BAL proposal.

The debate raged for four hours with much heat (if less light) generated by both sides. John Rodda, writing in the *Guardian*, described the debate as "*often vitriolic, personal and likely to leave lasting damage, deep fissures within the sport were laid bare."*

When it came to the voting, the Southern proposals were defeated on a show of hands (99 to 47). However, the South had done its homework, demanded a card vote (which would include proxies) and won by 783 to 583.

To those not involved in the politics of athletics at that time, it may have seemed incomprehensible that such passion could have been roused over the issue as, on the face of it, the advantage of one proposal over the other did not seem immediately apparent. It is also surprising that not one of those engaged in the debate saw the obvious compromise; that McAllister's formula should be time limited to, say, five years to enable the BAF to settle down and thereafter replaced by the arguably more democratic Southern alternative.

The problem was that, by this time, the degree of animosity between the various parties within the AAA was very intense and it became extremely difficult (probably impossible) for any of us to take a balanced view as every issue was seen through the prism of an entrenched point of view. With hindsight, it is possible to see that the Southern Counties, together with their leading lights, were genuinely fearful of losing their traditional influence in a larger organisation whereas others within the AAA were, equally genuinely, trying to introduce reform and were frustrated by what they saw as unreasonable opposition for the sake of it. It may also have been the case that ambitious individuals within England could foresee that, in future, the route to positions of power within the BAF would have to go indirectly (via the English AAA) and not, as in the past, directly from the regional associations. This would be an obstacle to be overcome by the English that the Celts would not face.

Whatever the reasons, McAllister had lost so, once more, it was back to the drawing board.

If the establishment of a BAF as a unified umbrella organisation for the whole of the sport was proving difficult, attempts were also being made to fulfil another strongly recommended reform, the merger of men's and women's separate organisations, particularly the AAA and the Women's AAA, the women's governing body in England.

COURTING THE WOMEN; WILL THEY? WON'T THEY?

It will be recalled, when I was describing the early efforts to persuade the AAA and Women's AAA towards reform, that, back in April 1983, the Women's AAA had been pushed by their member clubs into conducting a postal survey on the proposition that there should be a UK single governing body. The responses were overwhelmingly in favour and, accordingly, the Women's AAA, in November 1983, set up its own working group to study the matter.

The working group conducted its investigation along lines similar to the Turner Committee and came to similar conclusions. Its report was completed in March 1985 and accepted at the 1986 AGM of the Women's AAA. The report even hinted at the possibility of a merger with the AAA to produce a single English Association and recommended that the existing joint AAA-WAAA Working Party, that had been established to find ways of closer co-operation, be replaced by a joint steering group charged with working "*to establish a joint English Executive Council*". The Women's AAA did not foresee an outright amalgamation of the two associations but rather that an umbrella executive would co-ordinate their activities and the AAA and WAAA would continue in existence. This was not the full step envisaged by many but was going in the right direction.

Accordingly, the Women's AAA wrote to the AAA to suggest the joint steering group and, at its meeting on 30th May 1987, the General Committee of the AAA agreed. In fact, the committee that was created rejoiced in the name of "Joint Steering Committee into the amalgamation of the Women's AAA and AAA", implying rather more of a commitment than had been suggested by the women.

It was swiftly agreed that each association should be represented on the Steering Committee by eight persons (a mixture of officers, regional and specialist interests) and that an independent chairman be sought who would be acceptable to all. That person emerged in the figure of John De'Ath, a retired Air Commodore who was currently the Home Bursar at Jesus College, Oxford.

John De'Ath had been involved in athletics for 40 odd years, as an athlete and then as a leading figure in RAF athletics, serving six years as chairman of the RAF Athletic Association. After retiring from the RAF and taking up his position in Oxford, he became involved in the University

Courting the women; will they? won't they?

Athletic Club. He turned out to be an ideal choice for this delicate role; he was very well liked by the women's association and his quiet diplomacy and gentle steering of the committee paid handsome dividends.

The Steering Committee quickly got down to work and held its first meeting on 18th July 1987.

The leading personality in the Women's AAA was the long serving (since 1961) Honorary Secretary, Marea Hartman (pictured with Princess Anne), a formidable lady who had devoted her life to athletics and had become one of its best known, most influential and best connected. Professionally, she had held a senior position in the personnel department of the Bowater Group (international paper manufacturers) and spent all her spare time (and probably a lot of her professional time) on athletics. She had moved internationally within the IAAF as one of Britain's representatives for very many  years and had established contacts and friends all over the world. She had a particularly good relationship with the Japanese and was frequently invited to Japan, at their expense, for athletic occasions of all kinds.

Domestically, she was also the Honorary Treasurer of the Central Council of Physical Recreation (CCPR) and was on excellent personal terms with its President, the Duke of Edinburgh, who was also the President of the BAAB. This position was not exactly onerous as, some years earlier, in 1972, as a result of a deal involving a shift of some responsibilities, the CCPR had obtained from the Sport Council an indefinite guarantee to cover all its reasonable costs. The treasurer's duties, therefore, were basically to calculate the outgoings at the end of each year and send the bill to the Sport Council. She moved in all the right circles and few decisions were made by the Women's AAA without the nod from Marea.

Parallel with the establishment of the Steering Committee, "cordial discussions" were taking place regarding the possibility of joint AAA-WAAA track and field championships but this was not the change of heart by the women that might be supposed; remember the hilarity at the very idea when it was mooted back in 1975. ITV was criticising the poor quality of the exclusively female championships that were held annually in Birmingham in front of a mainly empty stadium and hinting very strongly that continued TV coverage could not be assumed. ITV wanted a joint

Courting the women; will they? won't they?

championship, as did most of the sport, and, under such pressure, the WAAA agreed that the first such championships would be held in 1988.

The issues to be resolved by the steering committee boiled down to finance, the management structure and the drafting of an acceptable constitution, but a thorny issue raised its head at the very first meeting; the anomalous position of the Welsh AAA. It will be remembered that the Welsh AAA (men) was part of the AAA whereas the Welsh Women's AAA had departed from a similar position within the Women's AAA some years before. It was immediately evident that the women would not agree to a merger with the AAA unless and until the Welsh AAA left.

Under the skilful chairmanship of John De'Ath, the committee worked well and progress was surprisingly swift and entirely amicable. The reluctance of the women simply to merge all their funds with the AAA was solved by my suggestion to keep 50% in a separate trust fund administered by the ladies for three years; the drafting of a constitution was not seen as a problem; some more work was needed on the organisational structure; and the Welsh situation had to be resolved.

The organisational structure was duly settled and a name for the new entity was agreed. The new body would be created by amending the AAA's constitution to embrace women, but exclude Welsh clubs, and its new name would be English Athletic Association.

Everything was now in place for the ground breaking merger of the AAA and the Women's AAA and all that needed to be settled was the position of the Welsh. However, it rapidly became clear that there was an impasse; the Welsh AAA would not secede from the AAA until there was a single governing body and the women would not merge with the AAA so long as the Welsh AAA remained. It was now the turn of the Women's AAA to express some irritation that the AAA could not, somehow, force the Welsh men out so that the amalgamation could go ahead (how things can change!) but resignedly accepted that this was a step too far.

By mid 1988 the steering committee had finished its work, issued its report and the scene was set for the merger. Assuming that the McAllister proposals for a BAF would be approved at the EGM of the AAA on 3 July, there was an air of quiet optimism that all the pieces were in place for the simultaneous merger of the AAA and Women's AAA and the launch of the long awaited one governing body on 1st January 1989 at the latest.

How wrong could they be?

Courting the women; will they? won't they?

As I have described, and much to the surprise of the steering group, the McAllister proposals were defeated and this struck a blow at the heart of its work. The Women's AAA had become wedded to the idea that, within the management of the BAF, a strong English voice was essential and that there would be no direct representation of the English areas. McAllister had proposed an outright majority for England on the managing council but this had been rejected in favour of English regional representation without overall English control.

This could become a deal breaking issue with the Women's AAA walking away from the table and, indeed, a new sub-plot emerged when the Southern Counties, through spokesman Derek Johnson, said that they did not want the Welsh AAA to leave the AAA at all. He could obviously see that, within the corridors of power, the South would be losing a political ally whose votes had often swung a controversial (indeed confrontational) issue in favour of the Southern position.

As the BAF project ground onwards the AAA-Women's AAA steering committee was re-convened to review its report in the light of developments. Bill Evans, once again leading the BAF negotiations, was invited to debate the thorny issue of English v Area representation but was unable to persuade the Women's AAA to change its stance.

The negotiations towards an agreed basis for the BAF would drag on for another two years and, under the chairmanship of John De'Ath, the Women's AAA gradually came to accept that the amalgamation of the AAA and WAAA was a desirable objective in its own right and that English representation on the BAF Council was a separate matter.

The Women's AAA focused more and more on the detail of the arrangements for the merged association and, perhaps wearily, accepted the inevitability of a BAF based on English regions.

BRING BACK EVANS

The animosity leading up to and surrounding the "McAllister v Southern Counties EGM" on 3rd July 1988 had attracted widespread condemnation as portraying the administration of a sport in turmoil and needed calming as a matter of urgency. The next opportunity to do this was at the AAA's General Committee meeting on 30th July at which the outcome of the EGM would be the leading topic.

Chairman Bill Ferguson appealed for a greater sense of responsibility and unity. He urged that, with the EGM in the past, the emotive election fever should be allowed to subside and that the AAA should aim to achieve an acceptable constitution for the new federation based on the decision of the clubs. He felt that the pre-EGM campaign had damaged the image of the sport by displaying an open split and that some of the language used in the publicity material "could have been more wisely chosen".

The implications arising from the EGM were the main topic of the meeting and, during the ebb and flow of proposal and counter proposal, one suggestion was that the Southern Counties themselves be given the task of producing a BAF constitution based on the six principles. Bill Evans appealed for sense, saying that to go down that road would lead to unnecessary delays and that the quickest and easiest course would be to amend the McAllister constitution.

Bill Evans' sensible proposal was eventually agreed to and he was asked to chair a new working group to take the task forward.

I was extremely worried that this public display of infighting could destabilise the sport's relationship with its commercial partners and, indeed, those of us who had been given responsibility for handling these matters (Promotions Officer Andy Norman, Financial Controller Malcolm Jones and I) were coming under great pressure, especially from ITV, to assure them that there was a stable management running the sport.

It was known that contract renewal negotiations were imminent and, in the heat of the meeting, a proposal was made to enlarge the negotiation group by adding Ewan Murray (BAAB chairman), Marea Hartman (Secretary of the Women's AAA) and Derek Johnson. This would have undermined the credibility of the three of us who had worked hard to built up a level of confidence with ITV and sponsors and, to my relief, was rejected by 13 votes to 8.

Initially, Bill Evans' working group made speedy progress but then became bogged down in issues of detail. The core question of the makeup of the managing Council continued to dominate and some of the specialist interest groups started to get into the act, wanting representation.

The depth of feeling came to the surface at the October 1988 meeting of the General Committee of the AAA when much of the meeting was taken up with arguments over the composition of the BAF Council. The Evans working group had initially suggested four votes each for the North, Midlands and South and five for the English AAA, giving a total of seventeen for "England" against eleven for Scotland, Northern Ireland and Wales combined. This proposal was actually carried by 13 votes to 11 but Derek Johnson stated that the South would not accept it. There was then a suggestion that the vote had not been properly counted and a re-vote was demanded; which resulted in a 13–13 tie. Chairman Bill Ferguson decided that, in such circumstances, he would not use his casting vote so the matter was not settled.

Feelings continued to simmer and the December 1988 AGM was an acrimonious affair with Bill Lucas, speaking for the Southern Counties, claiming that Ferguson had deliberately not used his casting vote in order to delay the introduction of the BAF.

John Rodda, respected athletics writer for the *Guardian* newspaper, could see what was going on. He wrote:

"The Amateur Athletic Association is going to fight to the end to prevent David Bedford and Derek Johnson gaining control of British athletics. After four hours of sniping during the AAA's annual meeting, from the Southern Counties Association and its many supporters on the one hand....."

A further twist of the political knife came at the January 1989 meeting of the General Committee, the first one after the 1988 AGM.

Prior to the January 1989 meeting of the General Committee, the Southern Counties challenged the right of General Secretary Mike Farrell to vote as an officer because he was a paid employee. This had never been questioned since Farrell had been appointed in 1982 and he was naturally upset by what he saw as a slur. Legal advice was sought on whether Farrell could vote but this was not conclusive. The intention when Farrell (pictured) had been appointed was that, even though a paid official, he would be a bona fide member of the general committee with a vote and this much was clear but the wording of the constitutional changes made at the time had left an uncertainty and the advice was that it would be safer if Farrell did not vote.

The first item of real business at the first meeting after every AGM was to appoint a chairman of the General Committee for the succeeding year. Bill Ferguson, who had been chairman since January 1987, was duly nominated by the Midland Counties whereupon Bill Evans was nominated by the Southern Counties and was elected by the narrowest of margins; 13 votes to 12.

The significance of the Farrell challenge was revealed as he would certainly have voted for Ferguson as the incumbent and there would have been a tie. A further curiosity of the constitution was that, in the event of a tie, the incumbent chairman (in this case Ferguson, even if he were not chairing the meeting) would have had a casting vote although whether it would have been proper to have used it in his own favour is another matter.

It seemed to me that the Southern Counties had taken this step (which some saw as sharp practice) as they saw Bill Evans as more sympathetic to their cause than Bill Ferguson. Ferguson had also probably paid a price for not exercising his casting vote as chairman at the previous meeting, in October, when the committee had split equally with 13 votes to 13 on the issue of the Southern proposals.

Bill Evans' election as chairman, and the manner of it, attracted criticism and Eric Shirley (former Olympic athlete and a Life Vice President of the AAA) stated his opinion that "*in his position as chairman of the [BAF] working party as well as of the General Committee, he (Bill Evans) would oversee the destruction of the AAA*". This was an extreme view but not unique.

After the bloodletting, it appeared that matters settled down a little and Bill Evans, now working closely with Derek Johnson and Arthur McAllister, did produce a draft constitution that, despite some reservations that it was a fudge and would not stand the test of time, met with general approval. By the early summer of 1989, enough progress had been made for the first draft of a BAF constitution to be circulated to all member clubs of the AAA and constituent members of the BAAB for comment.

But, although the general concept was acceptable politically, the financial arrangements had not even been discussed let alone agreed and there was still the tricky subject of the practical management of the new body to be worked out. This would prove to be far from plain sailing.

Having ousted Bill Ferguson as chairman, the South now had two of the principal officers who were sympathetic to their views but apparently saw me as less easy to be persuaded. As the only one of the leading group with professional financial qualifications as well as management experience, I realised the importance of establishing BAF as an efficient, well financed, organisation even if this took longer to achieve. This was interpreted as opposition to the project, which it absolutely was not, so they decided to get rid of me also.

Accordingly, in the run up to the following (1989) AGM, the Welsh AAA, supported by the Southern Counties, nominated the Welsh Treasurer, Dr Hedydd Davies, to oppose me. I had already been nominated for re-election as Honorary Treasurer by the Midland Counties AAA and by numerous clubs but it was also the prerogative of the General Committee to make nominations and this it proceeded to do at its meeting on 21 October 1989. Derek Johnson and David Bedford led an attack on me and the vote went 13:12 in favour of Davies. I walked out of the meeting in disgust.

A curiosity of the General Committee at that time was that two minor elements of the sport, Tug of War and Race Walking, were each entitled to send a representative with a vote. Thus these two votes sometimes held the balance of power and were often courted by protagonists, as happened on this occasion.

Ironically, in the morning of the same day, there had been a joint meeting of the AAA and the BAAB to receive a report on the negotiations for a new television contract with ITV. As I shall describe in Part II, these negotiations had been extremely difficult and had been conducted by Andy Norman, Malcolm Jones and me. Andy Norman and I had made the presentation to the meeting and were able to report that a satisfactory offer had eventually been negotiated.

Bring back Evans

David Bedford had said that "*he totally agreed that the offer was good and could be accepted*" and Eric Shirley that "*he was most grateful that we had such a talented team*".

There was widespread incredulity that the General Committee had not supported my re-election and, once again, John Rodda summed it up, writing, "*To the outside world this must seem a bizarre move...*" Ken Mays wrote in the *Daily Telegraph* that, "*Only hours after Mr Lister was congratulated... for his part in bringing the sport back from near bankruptcy more than three years ago, he was outvoted 13-12 in favour of Welsh Treasurer Hedydd Davies*".

During the 48 hours after the General Committee meeting, I received dozens of messages of support with countless urgings "not to give in". I also received a hand written letter of commiseration from Arthur McAllister in which he said that he had tried hard to prevent the coup and hoped that Hedydd Davies would withdraw.

Presumably fearing a backlash and in the face of a massive build up of support for me, Hedydd Davies did indeed withdraw his name 10 days later and I was duly re-elected as the sole candidate at the AGM on 2 December 1989.

I had known and been friendly with Hedydd Davies since we had competed together as Welsh athletes and, indeed, one of the most unsavoury parts of this episode had been that his nomination had been made by the Welsh AAA; and was made even worse by the fact that Bill Evans, as Welsh secretary, had himself signed the nomination paper.

I took the opportunity, during my financial report at the AGM, to publicly criticise Bill Evans for his part in the fiasco and was pleasantly surprised to receive standing ovation; while his wife, Kath, sat at the back of the audience quietly knitting. But Bill Evans' action created a rift between us that was never to fully heal even though it would not be a factor in our continued work together in athletics and towards the objective of a single governing body.

THE HOME STRAIGHT?

Work continued on perfecting the BAF constitution and this was now entrusted to solicitor Charles Woodhouse, a senior partner in Farrer & Co, a very distinguished and upper crust firm of London solicitors with offices in Lincoln's Inn Fields and who counted the Queen amongst their clients. Farrer & Co had acted as solicitors to the AAA for a number of years

Charles Woodhouse had acquired a large portfolio of sports governing bodies as clients and was well known in sporting circles. He himself had played cricket to a high standard. A tall, quietly spoken and resolutely diplomatic individual, Charles Woodhouse did not want to offend anyone and always looked for the compromise solution; commendable but not always useful as we shall see. He was already solicitor to the AAA and the BAAB and also advised the Women's AAA.

He was now asked also to act for the putative British Athletic Federation, creating the possibility of conflicts of interests as the respective interests of, in particular, the BAF, the AAA and the BAAB would not always coincide, especially in the area of commercially valuable contracts. Charles did not see this as an insuperable problem and the sport was happy to accept it as, at least, there would be only one (and a trusted) solicitor co-ordinating what was a quite complicated reorganisation.

Charles Woodhouse was preparing the legal formalities that would be needed. An entirely new company was to be formed called British Athletic Federation Limited.

It was to be incorporated as a company limited by guarantee (as opposed to having shareholders) and this was a conventional form for such organisations. As a company it needed a memorandum and articles of association. The memorandum sets out the objects for which a company is formed and this was straightforward enough. The articles of association define the way the company is to be managed and would need to contain watertight rules about the composition of the managing council and its powers, who were the directors, responsibility for the company's finances, who could vote and so on.

The AAA was already a company limited by guarantee but its existing memorandum and articles of association would need to be altered

The home straight?

to reflect its new status as the (merged men and women's) body for England only. To achieve this, an entirely new memorandum and articles were drafted to replace the existing ones.

In addition to the company formalities, legal contracts were needed to transfer employment contracts and other rights from the BAAB and the AAA to the BAF and, last but by no means least, a contract between the BAF and the AAA of England was needed to define their respective ownership rights over events and championships such as the AAA championships and to address financial and other arrangements that would affect their future relationship.

It was important that there should be no inconsistencies between these various documents and Charles Woodhouse played an important role in smoothing all these out.

And, finally, in order to implement all this, formal meetings of the affected bodies would be needed and the proceedings of those meetings and the wording of necessary resolutions had to be scrupulously drafted.

This was a lot of legal work and Farrer & Co, as a major London firm, were eye wateringly expensive. The legal costs alone for seeing this exercise through to its conclusion would amount to approximately £150,000.

Because the re-organisation would involve the transfer of valuable commercial contracts and other rights from the names of the AAA and the BAAB into that of the BAF, it was essential to take care that this would not attract unwanted tax liabilities. Expert tax advice was taken and Farrer & Co, with the assistance of the auditors, Alliotts, and overseen by me as Honorary Treasurer, obtained the vital official clearances from the Inland Revenue, without which the establishment of the BAF could not have gone ahead in the form desired.

As steady progress was now being made, a target date of 1st April 1991 was set for the official start of the BAF and this now began to look as if it was achievable. It would mean that the formal enabling meetings would all have to be held and all contracts signed off a few days before.

The whole debate had by now taken on a different tone; this time it was serious and all interested parties took a closer interest in what was being proposed.

The home straight?

A particularly ticklish issue related to the future AAA of England.

Until the infamous "Southern Counties EGM", drafting had proceeded on the basis that the managing Council of the BAF would include representatives of the four home countries of the UK and that the existing three regions of England would be represented through the AAA of England - they would not have direct representation. The logic of the decision taken by the clubs at the "Southern EGM" should have been that England as such would not be represented and that the three English regions would take their places on the Council alongside Scotland, Wales and Northern Ireland.

This is not what happened as direct regional representation was added to the existing formula and England was kept in as well. This replicated the Welsh anomaly on the BAAB, where the Welsh men had both a direct seat and indirect representation through the AAA; which was regarded as wrong and had been addressed by the Turner Committee. It also gave rise to the more practical dilemma as to the function of the AAA of England as the regional responsibilities within England would be devolved directly from BAF to the three regional associations and not to the English AAA.

It could be seen that there would need to be an exclusively English entity to select and manage the English Commonwealth Games team every four years and to arrange various English championships (but not the main AAA Championships as this would be handled by BAF through its commercial remit), but what else?

Bill Evans explained that England's role would be a "co-ordinating role" within England. It was hardly necessary to maintain all the paraphernalia of a AAA of England to fulfil this co-ordinating role but, by now, it would have been an impossible task to persuade the AAA to vote itself out of existence.

A curious consequence of this turn of events was that the English lost their opportunity to control the BAF. McAllister had proposed that the English votes on the managing Council (AAA of England plus the three regions) would out-number all the others put together (effectively continuing the "caretakership" that the AAA had conducted successfully). However, the formula eventually adopted in the BAF constitution gave the English only 20 votes on the Council out of a total of 47.

Nonetheless, with 20 out of 47 votes the English would be in a very powerful position to effectively dominate the BAF and it is surprising

The home straight?

that, as events turned out and as I shall describe, they chose rather to undermine it. When, at a later date, there was an external review of the deteriorating situation, the reviewer came to the view that those who represented the AAA of England were going through a sort of grieving process for the old AAA, which meant that their actions were driven by deep emotions rather than reason.

But this is to get ahead of myself as the BAF had yet to be born; and, at long last, the financial arrangements were being addressed.

It had long been taken for granted that the BAF would take over the lion's share of the responsibilities previously shared between the AAA and the BAAB and that, consequently, the major part of the financial resources then held in the name of the AAA would also be transferred to BAF.

As Treasurer, it fell to me to produce a financial proposal. This I did and presented it to the Finance and General Purposes Committee on 7th December 1990.

It was relatively easy to identify the respective responsibilities of the BAF and the AAA of England and it was readily agreed that BAF would handle all the commercial contracts with TV and sponsors as well as all other matters of a British nature, including the UK wide coaching scheme, international competition, rules, anti doping control, etc. From this it could be calculated that BAF would need a budget of around £2.6 million per year rising to £3m within 3 years. The equivalent figure for the AAA of England, now with much reduced responsibilities, would be around £250,000 annually.

I proposed that the BAF should be responsible for and retain all the income from the commercial activities (essentially TV and sponsorship income) and that this, together with other income of a British nature (Sport Council grants for coaching, for example) would be sufficient to cover costs and produce a surplus. I suggested that the AAA of England should receive an annual grant commensurate with its legitimate needs and that appropriate assistance should also be provided for the associations of Scotland, Wales and Northern Ireland.

In separate discussions, the Welsh men were to receive a "golden handshake" of £100,000 from the AAA in return for their secession.

The home straight?

Finally, I proposed that the working capital of the AAA, which was needed to cover ongoing commitments, should be transferred in full to the BAF, that £500,000 of the AAA's reserves should be retained by the AAA of England and the remainder transferred to BAF as initial capital.

As a result of the steps taken after the BAAB's cash crisis, the finances had been transformed. A combined AAA-BAAB pre-tax loss to September 1987 of more than £200,000 had been converted into a 1988 profit of £463,537, followed by further profits of £1.3 millions and £1.1 millions in 1989 and 1990 respectively. At the end of 1990, combined reserves (held and managed by the AAA) had been built up to close to £2.25 millions and these were expected to rise to about £2.7 million by September 1991, the re-scheduled start date for the BAF. This was a vast improvement on the position three years before but still on the low side to sustain the level of commitments that had been built up. I regarded these funds as having been created by "British Athletics" and that, logically, they should be passed over to the BAF; whilst making suitable provision for the legitimate future needs of the English association.

My plan would mean that the BAF would start out with reserves of around £2.2m. Against an annual budget of £2.6m, this was just about enough and something that could be built on.

The AAA of England would start off with £500,000 from the AAA plus an expected £100,000 from its merger with the Women's AAA and its annual outgoings would be covered by a grant from the BAF.

What, on the face of it, seemed to me to be fair and reasonable went down very badly with the AAA stalwarts. My proposals for handling future income and outgoings and the transfer of working capital were accepted without dissent but my suggested split of the reserves was described as "daylight robbery" of the AAA.

Arthur McAllister stated that *"the AAA has a right to its own money"*. Derek Johnson weighed in and disagreed strongly that *"the AAA should make such a gift to BAF"*. Ken Rickhuss (like myself coming from a business background), on the other hand, felt that it was *"unthinkable to start up a new business without a sound financial base"*.

Derek Johnson's intervention represented one of several "about faces" as, on an earlier occasion, he had written that *"it is important that our clubs, the public and bodies such as the Sport Council understand that*

The home straight?

we mean to give the federation our fullest support". He had proposed a transfer of at least £1 million when reserves were much smaller.

Bill Evans, chairing the meeting, was visibly shocked by the response.

As a counter to my proposal, David Bedford proposed transferring £½m to BAF with the AAA of England keeping the rest and making up any deficit during the first five years. But Geoff Clarke, an accountant, agreed that BAF would not be able to operate on only £½m.

And so it went on, in a tense and often angry argument over money.

Some of the English members of the committee had held a prior meeting and were evidently set on keeping as much as possible of the accumulated funds regardless of the effect on the BAF. With a majority of votes they could get their way and this they did, with the concession that to the £½m proposed by David Bedford could be added half any surplus made in the year to September 1991 and the amount of a development fund, which stood at around £500,000 but was ring fenced for specific purposes and not available to cover general costs. And, finally, the AAA of England offered to provide a financial guarantee to BAF for the first fifteen years of its life.

The BAF eventually opened for business on 1st October 1991 with a starting capital of £1.2m, one million less than I had suggested. Of this, the ring fenced development fund accounted for £532,000 and £200,000 had been placed in its charitable arm, the British Athletic Foundation. The AAA of England retained £1.4m out of which it paid £100,000 to the Welsh AAA. So the BAF's basic capital was only just over half a million pounds.

As John Rodda put it, "**BAF TO START WITH A LIMP**"

ENGLAND STILL NOT SATISFIED

By January 1991, sufficient progress was being made to decide a date for the various special meetings needed to formally approve the establishment of BAF. The chosen date was Saturday 17th March 1991 and the venue was Birmingham.

In anticipation, the legal formalities were put in place ready for formal approval on 17th March. The British Athletic Federation Limited was registered as a company at Companies house on 20th February 1991. A new memorandum and articles of association for the AAA of England were agreed as were draft contracts transferring assets from the BAAB and AAA to the BAF. The formal resolutions to be passed at the respective meetings (including those to wind up the BAAB and the Women's AAA) were drafted by Charles Woodhouse and all seemed set; except that the AAA was making difficulties over the agreement to be entered into by itself (the future AAA of England) and the BAF.

It will be recalled that the AAA had successfully built up a number of lucrative events. These were included in the joint AAA-BAAB television and marketing contracts and included the AAA track and field championships which were world famous and had been organised annually since 1880. For some years these championships had been used as the official team selection trials for the major international event of the year, whether the Olympic Games, World or European Championships or the Commonwealth Games. As the BAAB, and in future the BAF, selected Great Britain teams and organised the trials whereas the AAA championships belonged to the AAA, there was a mixture of rights to this event that had to be unravelled. The AAA had insisted that, whereas they accepted that, in future, the BAF would handle the marketing and organisation of all the TV events, the rights of ownership over the AAA Championships would stay with the AAA of England and they would expect to have a say in these matters.

This was a not unreasonable position but the relationship between the AAA of England and BAF needed to be documented in a formally binding contract so as to avoid the possibility of disputes in the future. Not for the first time, agreement proved problematic and, for the first time, Charles Woodhouse found his role in advising both parties to the contract extremely difficult.

England still not satisfied

The matter came to a head at a meeting of the AAA's F & GP Committee on 21 February 1991 when Bill Evans opened the meeting by stating his concern that the AAA was introducing into the draft BAF-AAAE contract new concepts that were at odds with the principles on which the AAA and BAAB members had agreed to go ahead with the BAF. He was clearly concerned that, with a date set and promises made publicly, these issues might, once again, undermine the whole project; this time permanently. He wanted to know why over-complicated financial mechanisms were being introduced by England into the contract and, more fundamentally, why the promised AAA of England financial guarantee to BAF was to be withdrawn.

In a somewhat contrived argument, Derek Johnson claimed that *"the AAA will no longer support a relationship whereby it hands over the negotiation of its contracts"* and that they were now merely *"prepared to discuss the question of the guarantee"*. Here was the potential to destroy the very basis of BAF and, as I pointed out, if BAF did not have the clear authority to negotiate with TV and sponsors, it had no future.

The meeting ended without matters being finally resolved except that one thing had been confirmed - there would be no guarantee; and the remaining conditions needed further work.

With time running out, both sides were forced to compromise and an agreement was eventually achieved.

The AAA used its muscle to extract terms that were very much in its own favour and which were to generate resentment in years to come as the AAA of England added to its own financial reserves at BAF's expense.

The agreement, as finally settled, would regulate affairs between the BAF and AAA of England, was to run for 15 years and then continue for successive five year periods unless either party opted out. It defined which events belonged to BAF and which to the AAA of England and what were regarded as the legitimate income and expenditure of BAF. Importantly, it specifically stated that all the income from the commercially valuable events would go to BAF which would also have the right to negotiate television and sponsorship contracts. So far so good but the sting in the tail was that 40 per cent of BAF's annual surplus after tax was to be paid over to the AAA of England, 10 per cent to the three Celtic associations and BAF was to retain only half.

England still not satisfied

In due course, some details of the agreement, particularly those relating to the method of sharing of surpluses, proved to be impracticable and were changed by mutual agreement but, over the succeeding years, the AAA of England was able to add significantly to its own cash balances and would prove to be unwilling to help the BAF when the need arose; as it did with a vengeance.

THE TICKING TIME BOMBS

In all of the debates and arguments over the formation of a BAF, the most controversial had been the composition of the management; this was a bare knuckled power struggle.

Turner had proposed a fairly simple four way split between England, Scotland, Wales and Northern Ireland, with votes to reflect their relative sizes, plus a federation chairman and six chairmen of committees that would represent functional areas of responsibility (finance, coaching, promotions, international affairs, domestic affairs and general purposes).

This had been rejected immediately by the AAA that preferred direct representation from the English areas. The Evans committee, however, reverted to the English only formula and this was followed when McAllister attempted to complete the work that Evans had started. McAllister was then overturned at the "Southern Counties EGM".

And so the ultimate formula written into the BAF constitution was that there would be a managing Council consisting of the following:

President	1 vote
Chairman	1 vote
Vice-Chairman	1 vote
Honorary Secretary	1 vote
Honorary Treasurer	1 vote
Representatives of the AAA of England	5 votes
Representatives of Scottish Athletics*	5 votes
Representatives of Welsh Athletics*	3 votes
Representatives of Northern Ireland Athletics*	3 votes
Representatives of Northern Counties Athletics*	5 votes
Representatives of Midland Counties*	5 votes
Track & Field Commission – chairman	1 vote
Track & Field Commission – hon. Secretary	1 vote
Cross Country Commission – chairman	1 vote
Cross Country Commission – hon. Secretary	1 vote
Road Running Commission – chairman	1 vote
Road Running Commission – hon. Secretary	1 vote

The ticking time bombs

Race Walking Commission – hon. Secretary   1 vote
Fell & Hill Running Commission – hon. secretary   1 vote
Tug of War Commission – hon. Secretary   1 vote

International Athletes   2 votes

It was expected that joint men/women organisations would be formed and, pending this, it was up to the existing separate entities how the votes would be shared.

A total of 47 persons, representing all the branches of the sport, could, and did, attend meetings of the Council and were entitled to vote; and these did not include life members and professional staff who would attend but not vote.

Whereas the Area Associations of England had got their way with direct representation on the Council, as I have already pointed out, England collectively, with 20 votes out of 47, did not have the inbuilt majority that, at one stage, had been mooted.

Such a group was far too large to meet very often and to efficiently manage the affairs of the federation and oversee the professional staff. Thus it met only a few times a year and the effective management was entrusted to a smaller management board.

And herein was created one of the fatal flaws that were to undermine the BAF.

The Management Board comprised ten persons; the five officers plus five others, three of whom would be appointed by the Council and two elected at each AGM. These ten persons were designated as the directors of the company (BAF Limited) for legal purposes and, as such, bore the weight of the responsibilities imposed by company law. It was the directors who, legally, were responsible for conducting the business and financial affairs of the BAF in a proper manner and, given the size and complexity of the commercial activities undertaken, these were obligations that had to be taken seriously.

The problem was that, written into the Articles of Association of the BAF, it was the Council which had the final say on all management matters and could over-rule the Management Board. The Management Board was therefore in the highly unsatisfactory position that it could be second guessed on decisions that it had taken in good faith. This did indeed lead to

The ticking time bombs

tensions between the Council (which was jealous of its rights) and the Management Board and, from time to time, boiled over into outright hostility.

I was familiar with company procedures and drew this discrepancy to the attention of solicitor Charles Woodhouse with a plea that he advise a clearer division of responsibilities. Woodhouse was sympathetic to the point I was stressing and that I was fearful it would lead to conflict. He was respected and I believe that his advice would almost certainly have been accepted but he declined to intervene, taking the view that it was up to the sport to decide on how it wanted to manage its affairs; a great pity.

A further problem that exacerbated an already delicate situation was the number of different hats that individuals would wear depending on the forum. So it was, for example, that a management board member, having participated in a decision as a member of the management board, could attend a Council meeting as a representative of, say, a regional association and vote with his colleagues on the same subject in a completely different way.

A second flaw was built into the very raison d'être of the BAF itself.

It was widely assumed that the BAF was set up as the governing body of athletics in the UK. For it to be able to deliver this effectively the BAF needed the power to make decisions and, if necessary, to insist on its decisions prevailing if there should be a difference of opinion within the sport. Such a power was not only omitted from the BAF's constitution but the opposite was written in.

The objects contained within the Memorandum of Association specifically limited BAF's role to "*the United Kingdom and international affairs of Athletics*", leaving open the possibility to argue that regional affairs were not the business of the BAF. Furthermore, the objects went on to say that BAF should "*secure, as far as possible, a uniform policy......in the UK and....to co-operate with National, Regional... Associations and to accept any functions....transferred....to the Federation on such terms as may be agreed between the respective National, Regional Associations and the Federation.*"

This was hardly a ringing endorsement of a new, powerful, body and contrasted with the old constitution of the AAA wherein the Area Associations were under the jurisdiction of the General Committee of the AAA.

The ticking time bombs

These weaknesses were brought to the attention of the General Committee of the AAA when it was debating the BAF's constitution and, not surprisingly, were rejected. It is not often that turkeys vote for Christmas and, as the majority of the members of the General Committee represented what would be regional associations within BAF, they were not likely to support a potential reduction of their powers.

A harmonious relationship between the Council and the Management Board and between the Council and the Regional Associations (particularly the South of England) was never achieved for any great length of time.

BAF IS BORN

The 17th March 1991 finally dawned and the many and varied representatives of athletics made their ways to the Vaughan Jeffries lecture theatre, University of Birmingham for the historic occasion.

The carefully choreographed programme saw a series of interlocking EGMs.

At the EGM of the AAA, the organisational and financial arrangements were explained to the assembled clubs' delegates and the formal resolutions were passed without trouble. Likewise, the BAAB and the Women's AAA voted through their respective demises and the celebrations could begin.

The athletics writers were generally positive.

John Rodda's article in the *Guardian* the day before had noted that "*the AAA is holding on to much of its power and authority, albeit under the new name of the AAA of England*" His article had been headed "**AAA holds on to a 15-year guarantee**" and he remarked that the BAF "*was not the sleek body envisaged*". As we have already noted, an earlier article of his had been headlined "*BAF to start with a limp*". Prophetic words indeed.

Everything was now in place for the BAF to start business proper on 1st October 1991 and there was a six months period during which the planning could be finalised.

During this period a small interim board of directors was appointed. The "interim steering directors" were McAllister (President designate), Evans (Chairman designate), Lister (Treasurer designate), Marea Hartman (chairman of the BAAB) and Margaret Oakley (chairman of the Women's AAA). Mike Farrell would act as secretary to the board. Subsequently, Geoff Clarke, David Cropper and Jim McInnes were added as interim directors.

Most of the deliberations of the interim board were of a mundane nature but it did, at least, finally decide that a new organisation needed a new management style and that this meant a Chief Executive, a position that had been long mooted but always postponed. Unfortunately, but true to form, the interim board itself failed to adopt "a new management style"

BAF is born

and missed the opportunity during the period from March 1991 to involve the senior professional staff in any of its discussions. This omission strained relationships with the staff who, understandably, were unsure of their own positions within the new organisation. Belatedly, the staff was brought up to date but some damage was done and it did not augur well for the future.

A Chief Executive, rather than a General Secretary, had been suggested as long ago as 1968 and it was hoped that the appointment would represent a shift to a more modern, streamlined organisation with direct line responsibility for the professional staff. This would represent a huge change of culture as, hitherto, even within what had, in practice, already become a single enterprise as a result of the AAA's caretakership, the Director of Coaching was responsible to the BAAB chairman, the Promotions Officer to the Joint Standing Committee, the Financial Controller to the Honorary Treasurer, and the General Secretary to the AAA General Committee. In other words, it was a mess that badly needed sorting out.

With the sport now turning in profits, the bill for corporation tax had also been mounting and in the two years 1989 and 1990, no less than £900,000 was taken by the Chancellor of the Exchequer in corporation tax. A more tax efficient way of managing the finances was needed to mitigate this heavy drain of monies that could otherwise be invested within the sport.

As part of the planned formation of the BAF, a charitable foundation, the British Athletic Foundation, was registered. The Federation and the Foundation would work closely together, with the foundation taking on many of the qualifying developmental programmes for the sport. The Foundation was to be funded by the Federation and any surplus profits could also be paid over to the Foundation and thus save the corporation tax that would otherwise be payable by the BAF. This was a completely legal and efficient way of managing the finances of the BAF and was copied by the AAA of England which established its own charity, Athletics for the Young.

The end (or, rather, the beginning) was, however, in sight and the BAF duly opened for business on 1st October 1991.

The new BAF Council held its first meeting in Birmingham on 6th October 1991 with 47 persons present and the first officers were appointed:

BAF is born

    President: Arthur McAllister

    Chairman: Bill Evans
    Vice-Chairman: Les Jones
    Honorary Treasurer: John Lister
    Honorary Secretary: David Bedford

There was some discussion as to whether Mike Farrell, the General Secretary (a professional position), should be appointed as the company secretary (a legally required position) and whether, in addition, there should be an honorary secretary. Tradition, and politics, prevailed and David Bedford was appointed as honorary secretary and became the company secretary also.

The membership of the Management Board was also settled and the five members in addition to the officers were Ian Clifton (representing cross country), Alan Warner (representing road running), Gordon Wright, Norma Blaine and Derek Johnson.

The mood at the first meeting of the new Council was upbeat with much talk of a new beginning, the end of old divisions, working together for the good of the sport, and so on.

How long would it last?

In parallel, the AAA, having changed its name to AAA of England, put in place its own new organisation. At the first meeting of its General Committee, in October 1991, Marea Hartman was elected President, with David Cropper as Chairman, Geoff Clarke as Honorary Treasurer and Derek Johnson as the new Honorary Secretary.

In Part II, I will describe the ways that the management of the business of the sport developed following the big change in fortunes in 1985 and how the BAF ultimately failed.

THE BUSINESS OF ATHLETICS

Introduction

Since the end of the nineteenth century, organised athletics in Britain had been an amateur sport, managed by amateurs. For decades it operated on a shoestring, depending on a mixture of handouts from the public purse and unpredictable profits from international matches. There were some good times, with matches at London's White City stadium in the 1950s attracting full houses, but interest in athletics started to decline and, despite the introduction of sponsorship (the first sponsored AAA championships were held in 1961), by 1967 the AAA was deeply in the red and facing possible bankruptcy.

Some professional expertise had been introduced - the first paid coach, Geoffrey Dyson, had been appointed in 1947 and John Martell was appointed as National Administrator by the AAA in 1973 – but the sport remained dependent on honorary administrators, many of whom, it must be said, were highly capable and experienced.

There was a resurgence of interest in the sport in the 1970s with the arrival of larger than life characters such as David Bedford, who set the Crystal Palace crowd alight with his world record breaking 10,000m run in 1973. Brendan Foster and Ian Stewart were winning medals and hard on their heels came superstars such as Sebastian Coe, Steve Ovett, Daley Thompson, Tessa Sanderson, Fatima Whitbread, Steve Cram and David Moorcroft.

This burst of interest, however welcome, did not immediately translate into commercial success and, although finances were easier, the BAAB was underfunded and, by the mid 1980s, had reserves of only £147,000 to service an annual expenditure of over half a million pounds; and remained dependent on public grants to pay for its professional coaches and international competition. The AAA, with fewer fixed commitments than the BAAB, had managed to accumulate reserves of around £300,000.

A major breakthrough came in 1985 when ITV outbid the BBC for the rights to televise athletics in Britain.

The business of athletics

In the words of London Marathon founder Chris Brasher at the 1984 AGM of the AAA, "*athletics had won the pools*".

And so it seemed.

In their accounts for the year ended 31 March 1985, the AAA and the BAAB had included income from television rights fees of £57,332 and £190,876 respectively. ITV's winning bid meant that the AAA and BAAB's combined income from television leapt more than eightfold, to £2.1 million per year, guaranteed for five years. And this was not all as the deal with ITV greatly improved the potential for income from sponsors, which should be the icing on the cake. The sponsorship selling rights were contracted to Alan Pascoe's company APA as he had guaranteed that the net income over the same five year period would be not less than £3m. Thus the sport had an assured income for five years, provided that it continued to promote televised events of the right quality.

Athletics was now riding the crest of a wave (what Tony Ward, in his book of the same name, described as *The Golden Decade*) with superstar athletes and undreamed of income.

What could possibly go wrong?

Let's go back a while.

In 1985, with the advent of big money from TV and sponsors, the AAA and BAAB could be rightly satisfied that they had capitalised on the renown of Britain's successful athletes in a big way. But such a huge expansion in the commercial activities of the sport needed a totally new approach to its management. Arthur McAllister and Bill Evans, who were the chairmen of the AAA and BAAB respectively, recognised this but lacked the business and management skills to introduce an effective system. They did at least realise that Andy Norman, the brains behind the increasingly popular events, needed to be tied in with a formal contract (indeed, ITV had demanded it) and he became the paid Promotions Officer, engaged jointly by the AAA and the BAAB.

To manage what were quite complex contracts with ITV and APA, the AAA and the BAAB established the Joint Standing Committee (JSC), a (thankfully small) group comprising the three officers of the AAA and the BAAB respectively.

The business of athletics

The JSC was set up simply to manage the commercial events but the overall effect of the huge increase in the monies flowing into athletics was likely to be felt throughout the sport. Expectations were high that funds would be available to do more than ever before to expand and develop; more coaches, more help to clubs, a higher public profile, etc., etc. However, little was done to prepare the general management of the AAA or the BAAB for the anticipated increase in workload. The attitude seemed to be that not much needed to change.

As an example, the day to day responsibility for handling the greatly increased amount of money was deputed to a part time clerical assistant who had little book keeping training. The person concerned was, in fact, extremely conscientious, possessed a remarkable degree of common sense and, given her background, did an excellent job. In an attempt to give her professional support, a part time overseeing role was contracted to a qualified accountant whose duties were to maintain the books correctly and prepare the annual accounts.

For reasons that I will come to, reconciling the financial figures was a nightmare and our poor, part time, financial manager who had done her best to cope with it described the situation in a lengthy memo dated 1st December 1986 to Mike Farrell, the General Secretary of the AAA, after she had been struggling to finalise the accounting figures to the end of September, as causing *"endless complications throughout the year and we need a much clearer and concise way"*.

It was hardly surprising that David Cropper, by profession a civil engineer who had been elected to the post only 12 months before and who had inherited this hornet's nest, should decide that he did not want to continue. Having been elected in his place, I discovered just how bad the situation was when I visited the Francis Street, London, offices of the AAA and the BAAB a few days later. Despite having the professional knowledge to tackle the problem it would take me quite a long time to fully get to the bottom of what had been going on.

I quickly realised that not only was the book-keeping system a mess but that, more seriously, there was no effective financial management and costs were running out of control. In my first report to the AAA, dated 5th January 1987, I warned that the AAA-BAAB were *"living beyond their means and in financial danger"* and that a priority should be *"the establishment of satisfactory reserves commensurate with the levels of commitments"*,

The business of athletics

It was essential to get the finances under proper day to day management and one of my first recommendations was the appointment of a qualified accountant. Surprisingly, Arthur McAllister, as President, did not think this was necessary and advised me not to push it. However, the Finance and General Purposes Committee quickly agreed and, after a frustratingly long period taken up by advertising, interviews and the need to give notice to his former employer, Malcolm Jones was appointed as Financial Controller with effect from 3 August 1987; more than two years into the contracts but better late than never.

The growing importance of commercial athletics demanded a more business-like approach but good financial control, however important, was only one element in the modernisation of the management that was needed and which was expected to be introduced under the BAF. The caretakership of the AAA following the BAAB's cash crisis in 1987 helped to provide a necessary degree of stability and the JSC came to be seen as a temporary arrangement until BAF set up a permanent structure under a chief executive.

However, as we saw with the painful birth of the BAF, the road to a more professional management structure and style was to be equally difficult to navigate. At the same time as the sport struggled with this, the day to day realities of commercial life - organising events, satisfying TV and sponsors, relationships with elite athlete, etc. – could not be escaped.

THE JOINT STANDING COMMITTEE (JSC)

The JSC was set up by the AAA and BAAB to manage the income and expenditure and other obligations arising from the TV and marketing contracts that had come on stream in April 1985.

The six voting members of the JSC were the President, Honorary Treasurer and General Secretary of the AAA, together with the Chairman and Honorary Treasurer of the BAAB and the chairman of its finance committee, solicitor Robert Stinson who was also the Honorary Treasurer of the IAAF.

It was agreed that the chair of the JSC would alternate annually between the chairman of the AAA and the chairman of the BAAB and that all decisions had to be unanimous otherwise they would be referred back to the AAA General Committee and the BAAB Council for a decision. This unusual arrangement worked remarkably well in practice. It served to concentrate minds and I do not recall a single occasion when unanimity was not achieved.

To take full advantage of ITV's offer, the formal contract had included several events that were not actually organised by the AAA or the BAAB. The Southern Counties had agreed that its annual grand prix at Crystal Palace should be included, as had the Women's AAA for its championships. The British League's clubs' cup final, the Scottish and Welsh championships, Northern Ireland's Belfast Games and various others were also included.

In parallel with the ITV contract the marketing rights to the events had been awarded Alan Pascoe's company, Alan Pascoe Associates Limited (APA). To grant these rights to the untried Alan Pascoe (pictured with Sebastian Coe) was a massive act of faith on the parts of Arthur McAllister and Bill Evans, who were charged with the negotiations, but an act of faith that was handsomely rewarded as Pascoe's company actually raised more than £8m, more than double the  guarantee, and went on to successfully represent British Athletics for many years; indeed, at the time of writing, still is.

The joint standing committee (JSC)

Alan Pascoe had been one of Britain's most successful athletes in the 1970s, including taking the gold medals for 400m hurdles at both European Championships and Commonwealth Games. Even while still a student and competing, he had dabbled with event promotion, helping to direct the Philips Night of Athletics at Crystal Palace. He subsequently gained more experience, commentating on athletics for television and involving himself in sponsorship of the AAA championships. With limited experience, but plenty of determination, Alan went head to head with the likes of marketing giants IMG and West Nally and persuaded the AAA and BAAB to give him the contract.

The JSC was responsible for managing the contractual and financial obligations and the actual organisation of events was deputed to a new entity called the British Athletics Promotions Unit (BAPU) composed of persons with practical experience of event organisation, under the leadership of Promotions Officer Andy Norman.

BAPU was responsible to the JSC which set the strategic parameters.

The first task of the JSC was to make an attempt at estimating the budgets for the first year of the contracts. Much time was spent in trying to work out a system for sharing the income and what emerged was a fiendishly complicated system of allocating points (each point having a money value) to the individual events that were to be organised so that, as the money was received, it could be shared out according to the formula.

The largest element in the costs of putting on these events was the appearance fees for the athletes and one of the key decisions for which the JSC was also responsible was how much they should be paid.

A few years earlier, in 1982, the IAAF had bowed to the inevitable and introduced a system under which athletes could be paid for competing. It had long been commonplace, but technically illegal, that the top athletes were paid by promoters to appear at their events and, the bigger the star, the bigger the payment, naturally. The AAA itself had connived in this deception by closing its eyes to what was going on at its own events.

Under the new system, an athlete could set up a personal "trust fund" that would be managed by his governing federation. His appearance fees would be paid into this trust fund and he could apply to the federation to draw out money to meet reasonable training or living expenses. The balance of the fund would be paid to the athlete when he or she retired. In

The joint standing committee (JSC)

practice, it was not uncommon for an official amount to be paid into a fund and an unofficial amount paid in cash. Not only this, but the definition of what counted as reasonable costs was so elastic that an athlete could pretty well do what he liked and, for example, payments for car purchases or mortgages were nodded through. It was a system that could not last and was eventually abandoned, athletes being treated just like other professional sportsmen.

Looking back to this period, subsequent generations of athletes are likely to find it hard to understand why this transitional arrangement of trust funds was necessary. Why not simply accept reality and immediately legitimise payments – as quickly happened? The answer lies in a mixture of tradition and sports politics.

It would not have been possible for a single country such as Britain to go it alone as athletics is an international sport and the rules are set by the IAAF. At that time, these rules decreed that athletics was an amateur sport and that athletes should not earn money from competing. Also, within countries such as Britain, the concept of amateurism had become deeply ingrained since Victorian times and the possibility of a move to "open" athletics was highly controversial and would have been anathema to many of the (amateur) administrators and officials.

Internationally, the IAAF recognised that the amateur rules were widely ignored but, in order to modernise their rules, needed a majority of votes at a congress of all the member countries to enact any changes. The IAAF was far from confident that a majority of countries would favour such a fundamental change as many, particularly those within the Soviet Union's sphere of influence, Africa, and some others feared that they would lose their control over their athletes and the income that they generated.

The Treasurer of the IAAF, Robert Stinson, who was a solicitor, came up with the idea of the trust fund, which would maintain the pretence of athletes not profiting directly (or, at least, immediately) from their performances and would also enable the federations to retain influence over their athletes. However, as I have mentioned, this was a system that could not last and, not many years later, it was abandoned.

In fact, sports historians will tell you that, prior to the advent of the Victorian "gentleman athlete", much of the sport in Britain had been highly professional with large sums changing hands from wagers and such like. Future historians may well conclude that it was actually the period of

The joint standing committee (JSC)

amateurism that was the aberration and that, by the end of the twentieth century, it merely reverted to what it had originally been.

Promotions Officer Andy Norman, who had been appointed to manage the TV events and negotiate with the athletes, lived in the real world and knew that there were market rates that would handsomely reward the top athletes who attract crowds to the stadia but offer next to nothing to all the others. (Norman had famously jibed to Linford Christie early in his career that he "*could not fill a telephone box*".) The JSC, however, thought that such a market oriented approach was unfair and proceeded to work out a set of "objective criteria" to govern the payments made to British athletes who competed in the British events.

The general idea was that all athletes would fit into a scale and be paid proportionally according to their status. As there was a going rate for the top stars the "objective criteria" inevitably meant that the lower ranked athletes received far more than they could command on the market and that the total cost of the package would be very high. Even the athletes' clubs were to get a modest cut.

The objective criteria would be applied only to British athletes as it was accepted that the payments to invited foreign stars would be negotiated individually by Norman according to the going market rates.

Based on these principles, estimates were made of what it would cost to put on the events scheduled for the summer seasons (it was initially decided that payments to athletes would not be made for the indoor events) but these estimates proved to be wildly optimistic and were overspent by a considerable amount. The "objective criteria" were eventually abandoned in the face of financial reality.

Having established the basic principles for dealing with the budgets, the JSC settled down to meeting regularly as it was responsible for managing all aspects of the contracted events, not just how much athletes should be paid. Unfortunately, this brave new world ran into a problem in the first months of its existence, with a dispute over political advertising at the Dairy Crest Games in Edinburgh in the summer of 1985.

A year earlier, the sport in Britain had been drawn into the controversial issue of South African apartheid politics when South African athlete Zola Budd had been fast tracked to a British passport. She had started competing in international events, including the 1984 Olympic Games, for Great Britain but was still spending a lot of time (too much it

The joint standing committee (JSC)

was said) in the country of her birth. A related issue reared its head in Edinburgh.

The rules concerning any advertising that could be seen on television were very strict and political advertising was forbidden. Contrary to these rules, Edinburgh Council had included a political slogan *"Edinburgh - Against Apartheid"* on their advertising boards in the stadium; they refused to remove them and ITV pulled out of the transmission.

This was not a good start to the TV contract and everyone was unhappy; Dairy Crest refused to pay their sponsorship, Pascoe's company was out of pocket, ITV threatened to withhold the rights fee and the JSC had egg on its face. The resulting insurance claim took a very long time to settle, by which time another dispute arose.

This time, ITV complained that the planned "Peugeot Talbot Indoor Games", to take place on 31 January 1987, was not good enough and, moreover, was scheduled for a different date from the one originally agreed. They would not, and did not, cover it. The JSC had, of course, decided that payments to athletes for indoor events were not necessary so, without a budget, Andy Norman was unable to attract athletes of sufficient quality to satisfy ITV.

By now, with the experiences of two disputes with ITV, overspending on payments to athletes and other organisational problems, the JSC realised that it needed to find a more efficient way of managing the contracts (especially the budgets) and asked the two treasurers to review the systems and come up with some suggestions.

The review of the JSC operations revealed that there was no real management of the budgets at all. Income had been divided according to the points system but there had never been any organised method of accounting for overall commercial income and costs. In particular, no serious attempt had been made to reconcile the separately prepared accounts of the AAA and the BAAB with the figures produced by the JSC.

To complicate matters, the AAA and BAAB had, in their wisdom, decided to change the ends of their financial years from 31 March to 30th September which meant that, instead of making up their accounts for a normal twelve months, an eighteen month account to 30 September 1986 was compiled, reverting thereafter to twelve month periods to 30 September. This made a true comparison year against year impossible for several years and was made worse by the fact that the TV and marketing

The joint standing committee (JSC)

contracts ran from 1 April to 31 March each year and the JSC compiled its own figures to these dates.

What became apparent, however, was that there was an imminent danger that, despite vastly increased income, the sport was starting to live dangerously beyond its means and it was this realisation that led in due course to the demise of the BAAB and its caretakership by the AAA that will be described in the next chapter.

Dealing with the BAAB's financial problems involved a great deal of pain and soul searching but it did lead to the necessary and radical overhaul of the management of the commercial activities that would result in a period of increasing profitability. The vital budget for payments to athletes was aligned more closely to market forces and the indoor events were included. Pascoe's company, APA, was mandated to bid for higher sponsorship income (which it did successfully) and, most importantly, Malcolm Jones instituted a system of budgetary control that could monitor income and expenditure on a continuous basis. The BAPU arrangement was scrapped as the JSC itself took direct responsibility for all aspects of the events.

Jones had taken up his position only in August 1987 so could have no influence on the summer season just ending, but when he produced the figures for the year the massive overspend on payments to athletes was revealed. The runaway train had to be brought under control; and quickly. This was done successfully and, together with other measures to increase income and control costs, bore fruit handsomely. Losses were converted into substantial profits and, by the end of 1990, the **AAA-BAAB** reserves had been built up to close to £2.25 millions.

The combined effect of the AAA's caretakership, the reorganised management of the commercially important events under the JSC and the introduction of professional financial expertise paid dividends but, at the heart of this financial success was the income and exposure provided by television.

As we shall see later, the relationship with ITV was proving to be more exacting than had been expected, with the initial groundswell of optimism and enthusiasm gradually being replaced by a more hardnosed attitude and focus on value for money that did not sit comfortably with many within the sport.

The joint standing committee (JSC)

After its initial teething troubles, and once the financial and budgetary controls had been introduced, the JSC settled down into what was generally an effective working unit. Andy Norman, Malcolm Jones and I were given the responsibility for handling the day to day relationships with ITV, Pascoe's company and sponsors and the JSC itself met regularly to manage the general strategy and to take major decisions.

The JSC continued until the advent of the BAF on 1st October 1991 when its role was taken over by the BAF's management board.

THE BAAB GOES BUST

The BAAB was a curious organisation. As explained earlier, it had been established as a hybrid to represent the UK internationally as the member of the IAAF for Great Britain. It was then given the responsibility for selecting and managing Great Britain international teams but was not provided with any funding from the domestic associations that had set it up. It had to fund itself and did this through a mixture of grants from the government funded Sport Councils and the profits of organising international athletic matches. In the 1950s and 1960s such matches had been the staple diet of international athletics but, by the early 1980s, public interest in them was waning and international matches were being succeeded by specially organised "grand prix" type spectaculars.

The AAA had shown some initiative in this area and, on its own and through the entrepreneurial spirit of individuals such as Andy Norman, Alan Pascoe, David Bedford and others, was tapping the emerging public appetite with some success.

Thus an unhealthy rivalry between the AAA and the BAAB (limited by its nature to promoting international matches) grew up and festered.

The BAAB had also been given responsibility for managing and financing a UK wide coaching scheme which employed professional coaches and this merely exacerbated the BAAB's financial situation as the coaching scheme was only part funded by Sport Councils grants and the balance had to be found from the BAAB's own resources.

As a consequence, the BAAB lurched between profit and loss without any solid financial base. The AAA, on the other hand, having passed its own responsibilities for coaching to the BAAB, was cruising nicely and declaring modest profits year after year.

As I described earlier, this imbalance had, in fact, not gone unnoticed by the Sports Council, with the result that an official enquiry into the financing of athletics was ordered by the then Minister for Sport, Neil Macfarlane. Not surprisingly, this enquiry was heavily critical of the way athletics was organised, at least from the financial point of view, and hinted strongly that a rationalisation of the organisation of the whole sport was needed.

The BAAB goes bust

But, in 1985, it seemed that a guardian angel had arrived that would solve all the sport's financial worries. The commercial broadcaster ITV decided that it wanted the athletics contract and was prepared to pay well to get it. A bidding war between the BBC and ITV saw ITV making an offer of £10.5 million for a five year contract. The BBC would not match this and so, for the first time in its history, the broadcasting of athletics went commercial. On the back of this TV contract, former Olympic athlete Alan Pascoe set up a marketing company (Alan Pascoe Associates Limited - APA) to challenge the likes of Mark McCormack's American giant IMG for the rights to sell sponsorship and other marketing deals. Pascoe offered to guarantee at least £3m of sponsorship over the 5 years and was awarded the contract.

ITV had made it clear that they must have exclusive rights over all the televised athletic events in Britain for the duration of the contract. In the face of such unimagined riches, even the diehards could see sense and the deal was consummated by the AAA and the BAAB jointly contracting with ITV. By a twist of fate, David Shaw, the former General Secretary of the BAAB who had resigned in frustration and who had also served on the Turner Committee, was now the General Secretary of the ITV Association and, in this capacity, responsible for tying up the formal contract with athletics. In those days ITV was composed of numerous separate regional commercial broadcasters and the ITV Association was needed to co-ordinate all their interests.

This deal, which ran for the five years from April 1985 to March 1990, forced the BAAB and the AAA to find an entirely new way of co-operating and, as we have seen, the JSC was established for this purpose.

The JSC then made the classic mistake of finding a complicated way of sharing the income and leaving the costs of staging the events to take care of themselves. It is true that an attempt to estimate the likely costs had been made but this was new territory for the sport and it could be expected that, for the price paid, ITV and sponsors would want commensurate (and expensive) quality.

There was also the question of who would actually handle the cash and it was agreed that all monies would be paid to the AAA who would distribute it in line with the agreed formulae.

Even before the ink on the contracts was dry, the AAA had announced in its January 1985 Newsletter to clubs that it would be

The BAAB goes bust

spending the riches on the development of the sport; a laudable objective but perhaps a bit premature.

Thus, the AAA and the BAAB slipped into a complacency, believing that their financial problems were solved.

Oh dear.

By March 1985 (before the start of the new TV contract), the BAAB had managed to accumulate reserves of £147,000 and in the financial year just ended had turned in a surplus of £34,000. With the new TV wealth coming on stream in April, the BAAB could reasonably expect to substantially improve on these figures but it simply did not happen.

Having changed its financial accounting period to match that of the AAA and end in September, the result for the 18 month period to September 1986 was miserable; a profit of a mere £9,000 out of revenue that had grown fourfold; and even this paltry result had needed a special transfer of £60,000 from the AAA to the BAAB.

These results were criticised at the AGM of the BAAB in December 1986 with Derek Johnson claiming that "*the sport was worse off than two years ago*" and Roger Simons demanding that the BAAB and AAA accounts be prepared on the same basis so that everyone could see the overall income and where it was going.

The AAA, for the same period, declared an after tax surplus of £107,000 (up from £60,000 the year before), itself hardly impressive given the rise in revenue.

The Treasurer of the BAAB, Mike Turner, prepared a budget for 1986-87 which revealed a potential surplus of a mere £1,300 and the realisation gradually dawned that the system of allocating revenues was not working. The BAAB believed that all that was necessary was to adjust the sharing (make it fairer!) in their direction but the problem was much more fundamental than that.

What had been revealed was the paucity of financial acumen within the leadership of the AAA and BAAB. They appeared to have been dazzled by the size of the likely income and had taken insufficient steps to put in place a full and proper appraisal of the essential costs that would be a first charge on the income (the costs of organising and promoting the events that generated the income in the first place). Nor had they recruited financial expertise to manage the money and control the costs.

When the AAA did its own budget for 1986-87, it too did not look very rosy and so began an investigation into the system itself. The two treasurers (Mike Turner and I; and I had been elected only a few weeks before and began to wonder what I had got into) were asked to compare figures and come to a joint conclusion on the situation.

The AAA took the view that the commercial income from TV and sponsorship should first be used to meet the costs of the events concerned. Out of what was left, agreed grants to the Celtic Associations (Scotland, Wales and Northern Ireland) should be paid and any final residue shared between the AAA and the BAAB in the ratio 2:1; and out of which the two organisations should have to cover their own costs. The 2:1 ratio was an assessment of the relative values of the AAA organised events compared with those of the BAAB and was, by and large, accepted as reasonable.

The BAAB, on the other hand, took the view that any final balance to be shared should be after specific amounts were allocated to the BAAB and to the AAA to cover their administration costs and that the BAAB's costs of coaching and its overseas international commitments should also be guaranteed.

All this assumed that the income would come in as expected and that the costs would be as estimated.

By mid-1987, the BAAB was running into cash flow problems. The AAA was paying over monies to the BAAB according to the old formula but the BAAB simply did not have enough cash to carry it through the period of the year (the summer season) when costs are at their highest. Panic phone calls were resulting in advances being made but this could not go on.

The BAAB Treasurer, in conjunction with the auditors, prepared an updated budget for the year which revealed that the hoped for surplus had turned into a likely loss of £283,000. This resulted from a combination of underestimates of costs in the original budget, lower net income from the promotions and inadequate cash flow. The writing was on the wall as the loss would completely wipe out the BAAB's reserves and leave it with an overall deficit of around £150,000.

According to the constitution of the BAAB each member association had to contribute to any financial deficit in proportion to the

The BAAB goes bust

numbers of votes held. Furthermore, the individual Council members might be personally liable for the debts as the BAAB did not enjoy the protection of limited liability as did the AAA.

A financial demand of this order would have placed some of the member associations into real financial trouble and the AAA recognised this. It was also conscious that it might not be forgiven if it allowed the BAAB and possibly the smaller Celtic associations to become bankrupt if it escaped relatively unscathed. There was also the worry of the knock on consequences with the TV and marketing contracts to which the BAAB was a party and which were crucially important to the AAA itself and the rest of the sport in Britain.

The AAA decided that it would have to shoulder most, if not all, of the burden and decided to propose that each of the BAAB members be asked to make a nominal contribution to the deficit and that the AAA would pick up the balance. This would avert a bankruptcy of the BAAB but, in return for this, the AAA would take over the BAAB's affairs and demand additional votes in order to have the power to manage effectively.

Two formal steps were the needed; a decision of the Council of the BAAB and a formal ratification of the constitutional implications at an EGM. The BAAB Council meeting, held on 12 September 1987, was a tense affair as much was at stake.

The AAA was represented by Chairman Bill Ferguson and Treasurer John Lister together with General Secretary Mike Farrell, David Bedford (South), Roy Mitchell (Midlands) and Charles Rice (North). The Women's AAA was represented by Norma Blaine, Jill Lindsay, and Margaret Oakley; Scottish AAA by John Brown, Bob Greenoak and John Hamilton; Scottish Women's AAA by Irene Docherty; Northern Ireland AAA by John Allen and Les Jones; Northern Ireland Women's AAA by Hilda O'Neill; Welsh AAA by Bill Evans and Hedydd Davies; and Welsh Women's AAA by Margaret Elgie. Chairman Ewan Murray and Treasurer Mike Turner completed the voting members.

Also in attendance were Life Vice Presidents Sir Arthur Gold, Arthur McAllister and Robert Stinson; two representatives of the international athletes, Joyce Smith and Mike Winch; and professional staff members Nigel Cooper (General Secretary), Mary Tupholme (Cooper's deputy), Frank Dick (Coaching Director), John Le Masurier (senior national coach), Conrad Milton (athletes' trust fund manager), Andy Norman (promotions officer) and Tony Ward (press officer).

The BAAB goes bust

The financial situation was explained in detail by Mike Turner and there was a long discussion during which numerous alternative solutions were suggested and, one by one, rejected as impractical. The inescapable fact was that the BAAB had run out of cash and was unable to pay its debts. To raise a bank loan in these circumstances (one suggestion) was felt not only to be unlikely to succeed but also irresponsible as it would serve merely to postpone the day of reckoning. Those at the meeting slowly came to the realisation that they had to put their own house in order and that meant finding extra cash from their own resources. The smaller associations were openly fearful about the likely consequences of a heavy demand on their already meagre reserves.

The offer from the AAA was explained and accepted by the BAAB Council, subject to approval at an EGM.

The AAA could have pushed much harder at the Council meeting and, given the demoralised state of the other members, could well have achieved an immediate decision to wind up the BAAB. This would then have given the AAA an opportunity to expand itself to embrace the remainder of the UK substantially on its own terms with the resultant single governing body that most by then seemed to want. Thus the arrival of the BAF (even if it might have been called AAA of the UK) would have been advanced by some three years.

Was this an opportunity missed? Probably it was but it may well also have generated such ill will against an "AAA take-over" that it would have been a pyrrhic victory. We shall never know.

And so, at an Extraordinary General Meeting, held on 10th October 1987, the earliest possible date, at the Grosvenor Hotel, Victoria, London, the BAAB bowed to the inevitable and voted to hand over the management of its affairs to the AAA and to allocate to the AAA an additional six Council votes.

The AAA's caretaker arrangement was expected to last only until the formation of the one governing body (target date 1st January 1989) but eventually continued for a further four years as the formation of the BAF was delayed, for reasons that we have already seen.

If the responsibility for this situation was placed on the shoulders of the BAAB, the truth of the matter was that both the BAAB and the AAA had been seduced by the income flowing from TV and marketing and had been progressively living beyond their means, being generous

The BAAB goes bust

with the money before it was earned. It was the **BAAB** that paid the price, perhaps unfairly, because the **AAA** had more reserves and was not burdened by the heavy costs of coaching and overseas international commitments.

Despite the fact that the **AAA** was now well in the driving seat, the **BAAB** carried on largely as before. Perhaps there was even a sense of relief amongst its Celtic members that they could continue to discuss international events, selection criteria for the Olympic Games, medical matters, doping controls, coaching and so on and so on, as well as going to international athletic events as team managers, delegates, etc. without having to worry about commercial contracts and budgets. All that could be left to the **AAA**.

MANAGEMENT CHALLENGES

The establishment of the AAA in 1880 had been at the instigation of a few enlightened Oxford University undergraduates and the pattern of management by honorary officials that they instituted continued for decades to follow.

Even as the sport had developed, in Britain as in the rest of the world, into the principal element of the Olympic Games and international matches and championships had proliferated, the amateur ethos, in management as in competition, ruled supreme.

After the Second World War, a generation of gifted and energetic administrators emerged to take the sport forward. Those such as Olympic champions Lord Burghley (Marquis of Exeter) and Harold Abrahams were giants on the domestic and international stages and were followed by the equally capable Arthur Gold, Marea Hartman and others.

The AAA was structured in a manner common to many sporting organisations with a President at the top of the tree alongside an honorary secretary and an honorary treasurer. A General Committee composed of the officers and representatives of regional and specialist interests would meet infrequently to deliberate and decide upon policy matters and then there would be multiple committees to deal with the detail of managing a national sport. All these groups would consist of elected honorary members.

The BAAB was similarly structured but tailored to its international and other responsibilities.

Even though, over time, an office had been established and some professional appointments made, notably the employment of professional national coaches, the power remained with the honorary officials. Within the AAA, the various committees were virtually independent fiefdoms, answering to the General Committee which met only a few times per year. The officers had considerable influence but even they did not actually have the power to command.

It is, perhaps, remarkable that such structures managed, for so long, to survive and prosper and the fact that they did is a tribute to the

Management challenges

prodigious amounts of time devoted to the sport by so many dedicated men and women.

It gradually became obvious that a totally honorary top management was coming under more and more strain. As the sport grew in importance it was far too risky to rely on good administrators becoming available through the old system and calls for more professional leadership became louder.

In 1968 Byers had strongly favoured the appointment of a chief executive but nothing had been done. The renewed impetus towards a single governing body that resulted in the BAF in 1991 had also reawakened the demand for better management under a chief executive.

The early mismanagement of the AAA-BAAB's TV finances which had led to the bankruptcy of the BAAB had also exposed weaknesses in the professional management structure. One gap was hurriedly closed by the appointment of Malcolm Jones as financial controller and, as we have seen, Andy Norman had been appointed Promotions Officer.

Thus, in the mid 1980s, the AAA employed a General Secretary (Mike Farrell) who reported to the (honorary) chairman of the General Committee, the BAAB employed a General Secretary (Nigel Cooper) who answered to the (honorary) chairman of the BAAB and a Director of Coaching (Frank Dick) who answered to the (honorary) chairman of the coaching committee. Promotions Officer Andy Norman answered to the BAAB for international matters, to the AAA for domestic matters and to the JSC for TV and marketing matters. Financial Controller Malcolm Jones answered to the AAA's honorary treasurer for AAA matters and to the BAAB's honorary treasurer for BAAB matters.

The Evans report on the formation of a BAF had been debated at length by the BAAB Council at its meeting on 14 February 1986. The report had come down against a chief executive, favouring the appointment of a "part time, paid, chairman" but, during the debate, a strong case had been made for a full time professional head to whom all the professional staff would answer and who would himself answer to the BAF chairman. Amongst those advocating a chief executive had been Andy Norman, the Promotions Officer. This case would be made frequently during the slow progress toward the BAF but, in the meantime, the sport's management continued as before.

Management challenges

One of the management nettles that needed to be grasped was the niggling that went on between Andy Norman, the Promotions Officer, and Frank Dick, the Director of Coaching (pictured with Olympic medallist Kris Akabusi). From time to time this niggling broke out into the open and was well characterised by athletics journalist Cliff Temple who, in 1987, described it thus:

Dick's responsibility is to lead a (British) team (to a major championship) at the peak of its carefully orchestrated fitness.

For Andy Norman, the priorities are different. He deals with individuals. "It doesn't matter if someone comes up with a points score at the end of the season showing we're the third best nation in Europe," he says. "The only people interested in that are the coaches trying to justify their existence."

Dick would prefer to see a computer system, fed with information from his network of national coaches, to establish a pecking order for international competition.

"I deal in practicalities," says Norman. "I come into the office at 9am to find someone has just pulled out of a meeting. So I get on the phone and try to find someone. I haven't got time to enter into long selectorial discussions"

The conflicts of interest between what Frank Dick described as the *performance* and the *commercial* sides of the sport needed an even stronger person to knock heads together and find the common ground as, there could be no doubt, Dick and Norman, in differing roles, were both genuinely trying to do their best for the sport.

Despite the fact that both the **AAA** and the **BAAB** employed full time general secretaries, these were regarded primarily as administrators and all major issues and controversies ended up with the (honorary) principal officers, usually the chairmen.

1988 was a typical year of mixed fortunes and unwelcome pressure.

Management challenges

In December 1987 *The Times* newspaper had run a three day series of articles on drug abuse in British athletics. Leading officials such as Andy Norman, Les Jones, Robert Stinson and Nigel Cooper were all accused of complicity in athletes avoiding the testing system and paying only lip service to the anti-doping regime. Robert Stinson was, at the time, the IAAF's Treasurer and was, therefore, in a particularly delicate and dangerous situation.

The subsequent storm that raged was extremely damaging to the sport's reputation and the AAA and BAAB had to take action. Advised by London solicitors Linklaters that a legal action against *The Times* could be ruinously expensive and with no certainty of success, the AAA played for time and instituted an independent enquiry chaired by Peter Coni QC.

No sooner was the doping scandal out of the news and starting to die down when another hit the headlines.

Zola Budd, a South African athlete, had decided to take up residence in the UK and her application for a British passport had been fast tracked through the system. She was therefore eligible to represent Great Britain in international competition and had, indeed, done so in the 1984 Olympic Games in Los Angeles.

In those days, South Africa was excluded from international sport as a protest against the apartheid system and anyone competing there was also excluded. The IAAF had been informed that, in breach of the international *Gleneagles Agreement*, Zola Budd had "taken part" in a race in South Africa and should accordingly be banned from international athletics. She denied this allegation on the grounds that she had not actually taken part in the race but had attended as a spectator and the matter reached the Council of the IAAF that, as it happened, was due to meet in London in April 1988.

The IAAF decided that Budd was ineligible and demanded that the BAAB undertake not to select her for Great Britain teams, failing which the BAAB could be suspended from membership of the IAAF. The suspension of the BAAB would have had far reaching consequences as all British athletes would, at a stroke, be denied international competition.

The legal advice received by the BAAB was that the IAAF had not acted in accordance with natural justice towards Zola Budd. The BAAB was thus caught between two unpalatable options; to defy the IAAF and defend Zola Budd or to acquiesce in the IAAF's demand and face possible legal

Management challenges

action by Budd. The BAAB decided to establish an independent Committee of Enquiry, chaired by Edward Cazalet QC and with members Marea Hartman and Ron Goodman, to investigate her eligibility.

Before the Committee of Enquiry could complete its work, Zola Budd voluntarily returned to South Africa and relinquished her right to compete. With a sigh of relief, the Committee was suspended and the issue shelved.

Later on in the same year, the BAAB controversially decided not to select Sebastian Coe for the Olympic Games in Seoul, thus denying him the opportunity to defend his 1500m title that he had first won in Moscow in 1980 and then won again in Los Angeles in 1984. This decision outraged the athletics press, generating headlines such as "Coe must Go", and the sport's leaders were once again under fire.

Both the doping and Budd issues had blown up almost simultaneously and placed massive demands on the time of the management of the sport. The chairman of the BAAB, Scotsman Ewan Murray, had to somehow meet the urgencies of the doping, Budd and Coe situations, with the whole of the British media on his back, while at the same time managing his full time job as an insurance underwriter.

And, if these pressures were not enough, trouble had been brewing over the latest BAF proposals and which had culminated in the "Southern Counties EGM" in July 1988.

The great hope was that the inauguration of a BAF would pull all these management strands together into a cohesive organisation and the pressure be taken off the honorary officers by quality professional management. To a very limited extent, some cohesion had been achieved when the AAA took over the management of the BAAB's affairs through the "caretakership" but this was only ever seen as a temporary arrangement, pending the formation of the BAF.

A CHIEF EXECUTIVE AT LAST

It had been accepted from the outset by most, if not all, that, under BAF, there would be a professional management structure headed by a chief executive and, as the discussions over BAF dragged on, so arose a growing call for the early appointment of a chief executive.

The professional staff understood the need for the "chief executive system" more clearly than most of the honorary personnel as they found it frustrating having to deal with so many "honoraries", some of whom could be difficult to contact if an urgent decision were needed. However, the "honoraries" were reluctant to grasp this nettle and continuously postponed a decision, reasoning that the BAF should make the appointment when it was set up.

The nettle was finally grasped by the interim steering directors of BAF who, at a meeting in 1991, decided to advertise for a chief executive, hoping that the position could be filled in time for the start of BAF in October of that year.

The advertisements were placed and numerous applications received. Interviews were held with the final short list of candidates, one of whom was the well respected and popular financial controller Malcolm Jones. Jones had been appointed in 1987 and had done an extremely good job in bringing the finances of the sport under control. He had established excellent working relationships with commercial partners ITV, Alan Pascoe Associates and sponsors and had introduced a level of commercial reality and financial discipline that had not previously existed.

As a former commercial director of Westland Helicopters, Jones had management experience and convinced the interviewing panel that he was the right man to be chief executive. In his four years as financial controller, he had got to know the sport inside out and, tellingly, was confident that he could weld together a good team, in particular managing the strong personalities and egos of Andy Norman and Frank Dick.

A chief executive at last

Malcolm Jones became chief executive of the BAF on 18 November 1991 and one of his first tasks was to recruit a new financial controller. This he did and Steve Gledhill took up his position on 27 January 1992.

Although Malcolm Jones had been an excellent financial controller, he was not an unqualified success as chief executive and, after only sixteen months in the post, resigned on 2 April 1993 in controversial circumstances which, perhaps inevitably, gave yet another excuse for political opportunism.

Jones' performance had been a cause of growing concern for several months and came to a head spontaneously at a meeting of the management board when a discussion led to a unanimous expression of a lack of confidence in the chief executive. This was a very delicate situation that needed to be handled quickly, sensitively and confidentially. Unfortunately, it was bungled.

The chairman, Bill Evans, who had been present at the meeting, was tasked with informing the President, McAllister, who had not been present, of the situation and with meeting Jones urgently. However, it was not until six days later that Evans met Jones, by which time the matter leaked to the press and ran virtually out of control. McAllister wrongly claimed that he had known nothing of the growing problem and Evans sat on his hands.

Throughout, Jones acted with dignity and, finding himself in an impossible position, resigned.

Suddenly, the fledgling BAF found itself without its chief executive and, for the second time in its brief life, it had lost a key figure.

Upon the formation of the BAF, Northern Irishman Les Jones (pictured) had been elected Vice-Chairman. Jones was a leading light in Northern Ireland athletics, where he was the chairman of the Northern Ireland Association, and was also the senior team manager of the Great Britain athletics team. A popular figure on the athletic circuit, Les Jones was tipped for a high position in European or world athletics.

On 2 March 1992, Les Jones suffered a fatal heart attack and was found dead in his hotel room in Genoa where he was leading the British

A chief executive at last

team at the European Indoor Championships. Les was only 48 and his death was a shocking blow to athletics in Britain.

Within six months of its launch, the BAF had lost its first Vice-Chairman.

The BAF did not lose any time in finding a replacement and, at its meeting on 26th April 1992, elected Peter Radford as Vice-Chairman.

Radford, a professor of sports science at Glasgow University, had been an Olympic athlete, taking the bronze medal in the 100m at the Rome Olympic Games of 1960. He had also set new world records for 200m and 220 yards and, to this day, remains the last British athlete to hold a world record at these distances. He was also a member of Britain's 4 x 110 yards relay team that equalled the world record in 1963 when beating the powerful USA team in an international match at the White City stadium.

Radford had spent some years in Canada as the Canadian director of coaching and, in recent years, had co-authored a report into the UK's coaching scheme. He was a respected authority in the field of anti-doping and, as a noted sports historian, his knowledge of the sport was considerable. He was a popular choice to fill Les Jones' position.

Within a year, Radford had stepped up to become chairman, following Bill Evans' decision not to seek re-election at the 1993 AGM of the BAF, and Scotland's Bob Greenoak had taken Radford's place as Vice-Chairman.

The 1993 AGM had been another bruising affair that, yet again, portrayed British Athletics as constantly warring with itself. The officers had borne the brunt of the Malcolm Jones affair and this manifested itself in the elections.

Radford, Greenoak and Bedford found themselves opposed by David Cropper, Ken Oakley and Chris Carter each of whom had, significantly, been nominated by all three English Regional Associations.

An effective lobbying campaign resulted in clear majorities for Radford, Greenoak and Bedford and the President Arthur McAllister, who had almost certainly been involved in this attempt to seize power, was visibly stunned when the voting results were announced.

A chief executive at last

An undoubted weakness of the BAF constitution was that all the officers were subject to annual election. This had been the same under the former AAA and a kind of competitive culture had grown up, centred on the annual election of officers at the AGM. Peter Radford, experiencing this at first hand, was concerned at the serious effects of this culture. He believes that it became a battle between rival groupings, not to elect the best person but to get "their man" into position. Winning at the AGM became an end in itself and the interests of the sport took second place. This attitude was evidenced at the 1994 AGM when both Greenoak and Bedford were ousted in favour of Eric Shirley and Matt Frazer.

During his brief tenure, David Bedford took his responsibilities as Honorary Secretary extremely seriously and was an excellent officer and ambassador for British athletics. In a spirit of goodwill, both he and I put past differences behind us and forged an amicable and effective working relationship. It was a pity that Bedford himself became a victim of political manoeuvring but his successor, Matt Frazer, a solid northerner, brought different qualities to the position and also did a good job.

Coincidentally, Derek Johnson had given up as Honorary Secretary of the AAA of England a few months before after only two years in the position so both his and Bedford's periods in key positions had turned out to be equally short.

Following Malcolm Jones' resignation as chief executive, a replacement was sought. The advertisement attracted numerous candidates and a short list was identified. These were interviewed by the interviewing panel but none quite matched what was needed. Radford, as the BAF chairman, had been one of the panel and left the final interview session to return home to Glasgow.

After Radford had left, the interviewing group continued deliberating over what to do next and the idea was floated to ask Radford himself if he would be interested in taking the post. He had been toying with the idea of a move from Glasgow and, although surprised to be asked, said that he would be interested and would think on it. However, he immediately realised that as he had been part of the interviewing panel his appointment might be seen as a "put up job".

A chief executive at last

When Radford confirmed that he would be interested in the challenge, the management board was apprised of the situation and enthusiastically supported the proposal, agreeing, at Radford's suggestion, that it would be better if he were called executive chairman and not chief executive.

The position of executive chairman had not been foreseen when the BAF's constitution had been written so an EGM was called to approve the necessary amendments. This was held on 12 December 1993, the amendments were duly passed and Radford made a short speech and received a round of applause.

At the same meeting, it was decided that there should be a separate chairman of the Council and Ken Rickhuss was elected to this position. Radford, as executive chairman, would chair the Management Board.

A POISONED CHALICE?

After an initial honeymoon period, the early years of the BAF were uncomfortable. Relationships with ITV were not going well and the commercial events were not attracting viewers or spectators as before. The controversy surrounding the departure of Malcolm Jones had reopened old animosities which polarised with the challenges to the officers at the 1993 AGM.

When he agreed to become the executive chairman, Radford (pictured) knew that he would be taking on a difficult task. David Miller, chief sports writer of *The Times* newspaper, penned a full page article on 16th December 1993 which laid bare the problems. After describing the successful world athletics championship in Stuttgart, where British athletes had won 10 medals including 3 gold (Linford Christie, Colin Jackson and Sally Gunnell), he wrote:

"*Athletics holds the all-comers record for post war mismanagement. A succession of weak, bickering or ignorant chairmen..... have allowed the administration to drift rudderless.*"

Miller went on to describe what he perceived to be the problems in the sport and the enormity of the task Radford had taken on.

Peter Radford took up his position as executive chairman on 1st February 1994 and immediately walked into a storm.

Andy Norman had long enjoyed a love-hate relationship with the British athletics press and one of them, Cliff Temple, had been preparing to write a critical article for the *Sunday Times*. Norman had got wind of this and had had a heated telephone conversation with Temple during which, it was claimed, Norman had threatened Temple. Sometime later, Temple, who had suffered from severe depression following the breakup of his marriage, committed suicide by throwing himself in front of a train and Norman had been accused of being, at least partly, responsible for his death. This Norman hotly denied but others of the athletic press saw an opportunity to get back at him and whipped up the controversy.

A poisoned chalice?

This was a potential disaster for the BAF as Norman was a key figure in delivering high quality events to satisfy ITV; indeed, many saw him as the only person capable of doing this.

The BAF could not ignore the matter as a public relations catastrophe was looming and it fell to the new executive chairman to deal with the hottest of hot potatoes.

Radford acted decisively by suspending Norman and commissioning an urgent enquiry into the affair, concluding that, whether the allegations against Norman were right or wrong, so much damage was being done to the BAF's reputation that Norman had to go.

Norman's employment ceased on 29 April 1994 and Ian Stewart, his deputy, took over as Promotions Director.

In the meantime, Frank Dick had resigned as Director of Coaching, citing likely budget cuts that would threaten his ability to do his job.

In late 1994, another bombshell landed when Diane Modahl, Britain's best 800m runner at the time, tested positive for a banned drug. She had been asked to give a urine sample after a race in Portugal and the sample had been tested by a laboratory there but, under the doping rules of the IAAF, it was the responsibility of the BAF, as the athlete's governing federation, to conduct the investigation and to apply any sanctions. Thus, as an innocent party, the BAF became caught up in the eye of a storm that would rumble on for several years.

The Modahl case developed into a "cause celebre" that was to occupy much time and consume in legal costs such a large part of the BAF's dwindling income that it came to be blamed as a reason for the financial demise of the federation.

The first hearing of the case went against Modahl but she appealed, as she was entitled to. Between the first hearing and the appeal the Modahl team managed to compile sufficient scientific evidence to cast doubt on the implications of the original testing in Portugal and the appeal panel came down on her side. She had therefore been "cleared" by the BAF but the IAAF, dissatisfied, announced that they would take the matter to arbitration.

A poisoned chalice?

The Modahls virtually bankrupted themselves with the heavy costs they expended on the defence and, in February 1996, sued the BAF for around £480,000 in an attempt to recover their costs and damages. Likewise for the BAF, the costs had absorbed some £200,000 of the BAF's already stretched resources and the drain continued as the legal dispute went on.

Diane Modahl's had been only one of a spate of British doping cases at this time and, although British Athletics was respected as being tough on doping cheats, the adverse publicity and attendant costs were harming the reputation of the sport.

The problems landing on Radford's desk were mounting and, at the same time, he was trying to look ahead and plan for the future. With the support of the management board, he undertook a wide ranging review of the state of the sport and produced a blue print for the future called *Athletics21 – Strategic Planning for British Athletics in the 21st Century*, which was published in April 1995.

He was also lobbying hard for a change to the rules for disbursing National Lottery funds which, hitherto, had been restricted to capital projects. He launched a bid for Britain to host the World Athletics Championships and gained the support of the government to commit to build a new national athletic stadium in north London.

In these endeavours, he achieved remarkable success and has not received enough credit for the pioneering work that he did and which has resulted in substantial National Lottery and Sports Council monies flooding into athletics since 1997.

Radford had inherited a declining income from television and sponsors which meant that budgets were constantly under pressure. This affected the whole sport and not least the athletes through their appearance fees. Some of the athletes did not take kindly to these "cuts" and relationships between them and the BAF deteriorated. One incident involving Colin Jackson sparked off others.

One of the most important events every year was the AAA Championships which doubled as the trials for the major championship of the year. No appearance money was paid but, nevertheless, athletes were obliged to participate as part of the qualification process towards selection. In 1995, Colin Jackson had competed in the heats of the 110m hurdles but

A poisoned chalice?

failed to show up for the final the following day, instead flying to Italy for a paid appearance in an event there.

Technically, Jackson had met the selection criteria by taking part in the trials but the BAF took a dim view of this as it felt that Jackson had short changed the spectators and damaged the principle of the trials. He was called to Radford's office where he received a dressing down; which he took very badly and vowed not to compete in Britain again. Later in the same year, Jackson, Linford Christie and John Regis, three crowd pullers, refused to compete at the important Crystal Palace grand prix and rubbed salt in the wound by strolling down the home straight in full view of the spectators and the media.

During this period, the BAF management board was wrestling with its budgets and, as Treasurer, I was warning that cut backs were essential if the sport were to live within its means. My appeals to create new income sources had fallen on deaf ears and, in particular, my proposal for a national athlete registration scheme which could have generated substantial income, and which was being demanded by the Sports Council, had been opposed by the South of England Association.

In fact, back in 1984, the AAA had successfully launched a national registration scheme and had built a membership roll of some 26,000. Unfortunately, the membership fee had been set at a totally inadequate £5 out of which insurance, physiotherapy and other promised benefits had to be funded and, as a result, the scheme lost money from the start and was abandoned after two years with losses of £70,000. This level of loss represented around £2.50 per member and if only a more realistic fee of, say, £10 (still good value for the benefits) had been charged the result would have been totally different and the scheme could have been developed to become a major source of income. A golden opportunity was sadly missed.

By now I had now spent the best part of ten, often difficult, years at the financial helm and decided that I would not seek re-election at the March 1996 AGM. Wearily, I stepped down as Honorary Treasurer and the South's Martin Evanson took over. At the same AGM, Arthur McAllister retired as President and the popular Mary Peters, Olympic pentathlon champion in 1972, was elected in his place.

I had mixed feelings about stepping down as, at long last, the BAF was making some serious attempts to address its financial predicament and Radford's lobbying to change the rules of the National Lottery

A poisoned chalice?

encouraged him to launch a bid to break the BAF's dependence on television based revenues. Firstly, an application for a £2m annual grant from the Sport Council for 1997 and onwards was submitted (up from £300,000) and, simultaneously, a £4.5m annual bid for coaching and elite athlete preparation was made to the National Lottery fund.

Whilst these efforts to provide a more secure future funding were being made, the current difficult financial situation was exacerbated when ITV failed to broadcast an event from Crystal Palace, preferring to screen a "soap", and then curtailed the coverage of an event at Gateshead. This meant that sponsors had to be repaid and a hole opened up in an already weak budget. This was made worse when another sponsor failed to pay, resulting in a bad debt write off. Thus a budgeted deficit for 1996 of a manageable £100,000 turned into an overall loss of £640,000 (BAF and the Foundation combined) for the year.

There was clearly a need to get a firm grip on a deteriorating situation and a plan to reorganise was developed.

To create a greater focus on where monies came from and how they were spent, the first part of the plan was to hive off the televised events to a wholly owned subsidiary company, to be called Concept Athletics, the management of which would be shared with the international athletes; thereby giving them a direct stake in the success of the events that were so important to them and to the sport.

Radford's conciliatory approaches to the elite athletes after the black days of 1995 had borne fruit and a new spirit of co-operation had grown, thanks particularly to the leadership shown by Roger Black and Geoff Parsons and supported by others such as Shaun Pickering. This work had been so successful that a new British Athletes Association was formed to represent the interests of the top international athletes and to work with the BAF. As we shall see when discussing television, this spirit of co-operation was to prove crucial in securing a contract with Channel 4.

The second element in the reorganisation was to set up a further subsidiary (Performance Athlete Services) to manage coaching and other assistance given to athletes for their development and to enable them to achieve their full potential. Encouraging sounds were emerging from Sports Council sources that a very substantial increase in funding may be forthcoming and the establishment of Performance Athlete Services would enable this money to be ring fenced and clearly identified.

A poisoned chalice?

The BAF itself would continue in its constitutional role as the governing body and would oversee and coordinate the activities of the two new subsidiaries. Hopefully the sports dependence on television based income would, at long last, be broken.

Radford had also ensured that athletics had secured a place at the table in the discussions about a possible National Stadium to replace the outdated Wembley Stadium. The inclusion of an athletics track would, for the first time, provide a stadium suitable to host a World or European athletics championship and, indeed, a bid to host the 2001 World championships was launched at the same time. This bid proved to be successful but was aborted when the Government withdrew its support.

But all in the garden was not rosy as, once again, the sport shot itself in the foot by rejecting a further attempt to create what was now seen as an essential registration, or membership, scheme. The Chairman (Ken Rickhuss) and Honorary Secretary (Matt Frazer) had made a huge effort to get the scheme off the ground, travelling to every BAF region to argue the case. Several regions had already introduced local schemes but it again proved impossible to extend these nationally.

The BAF, and before it the AAA and the BAAB, received a small amount of public finance through the Sports Councils and the vast majority of its income came from television and sponsorship income produced by its major events. Naturally, a significant part of this income had to be spent on the events that created it in the first place and, out of what was left, coaching, major championships teams, administration, development and support to regional associations all had to be funded. Opposition to membership or registration schemes had usually foundered on the misconceived belief that the monies raised would simply be channelled to the top athletes (*"who already took too much out of the sport"*). It had been the oft repeated desire to rid itself of its dependence on fragile income from TV and sponsorship that had driven the need for the sport to provide more of its money itself.

There was also continuing aggravation from the South of England Association and the AAA of England.

For years the Southern Counties had questioned the arrangements for their grand prix event which had been sponsored initially by Peugeot Talbot and called the Peugeot Talbot Games. When ITV had made its successful bid for the athletics contract in 1985, the South had agreed for this event to be included in the overall contract but the South had then

A poisoned chalice?

raised an issue that was never settled - that of the actual ownership of the rights attached to the event - and threatened to remove it from any future TV contract, thus potentially jeopardising the sport's relationship with ITV. Despite many efforts to reach an agreement over the issue, it turned into a running sore that soured relationships between the BAF and the South.

Then, in late 1996, when ITV had finally decided not to continue and the BAF was concluding highly delicate negotiations with Channel 4 television and sponsors for the forthcoming season, the South provocatively challenged the BAF to allow them to organise a second (televised) invitation meeting at Crystal Palace, to be called "The London Games". At the same time, the AAA of England proposed a change to the Rules that would allow any region to negotiate its own television arrangement; which would, at a stroke, have destroyed the BAF's ability to negotiate for the whole of the UK and risked a breach of contract with Channel 4. The AAA of England also refused to permit the BAF to incorporate the 1997 world championships trials within "their" AAA Championships.

The AAA of England had steadfastly refused to recognise that it was only the "trials" within the AAA Championships that had kept them alive. Athletes could not risk missing the trials if they wanted to be selected for the particular international championship but there was no such imperative to contest the domestic AAA Championship. History and tradition were no longer enough to sustain *"the AAAs"* and this sad fact of life came true with a vengeance in 1997 when the AAA of England went it alone. With no TV coverage, hardly any sponsorship and few of the top athletes taking part, the historic championships were a sorry sight in a virtually empty Alexander Stadium, Birmingham.

The infighting and general situation had deteriorated to such an extent that, when opening a meeting of the BAF Council on 18th January 1997, Ken Rickhuss, the chairman, felt it necessary to state that *"when he accepted the position of Chairman of Council, it was his hope to bring the various parts of the sport together. However this had so far proved unsuccessful and as a result of all the conflicts, he doubted that some people within the sport really wanted this"*.

At the same meeting, Radford reported that a contract had been secured with Channel 4 television for two years with an option for a further two but, when describing the conditions in which the negotiations had been conducted, said that *"this instability (the problems in the sport) is not driven by those involved in discussions with major partners but from others*

A poisoned chalice?

who seek, for whatever reason, to influence these discussions to the disadvantage of the Federation. The internal battle that has been fought behind my back was a disgrace to British Athletics and one which members should be ashamed of".

In January 1997, Steve Gledhill, who had done an excellent job for the federation, resigned as Director of Finance and, two weeks later, Radford also announced his resignation.

The last straw for Radford had been these attempts by those that he regarded as his own colleagues to undermine his negotiating position on behalf of the BAF with commercial partners. He came to the conclusion that as he could no longer trust some of the very people to whom he was answerable, he had to leave. He described it as feeling like a rugby player, with the ball in his hands, racing for the line, only to be tackled by players on his own side.

The resignations and subsequent departures of Radford and Gledhill placed unwanted pressures on the Officers and other honorary members of the management board, which they struggled to cope with. It fell to chairman Ken Rickhuss, an engineer and successful businessman, along with his fellow officers, to try to pick up the pieces.

At its meeting on 15 March 1997, the Council set in train the process to recruit a replacement for Radford, aiming to have the successful candidate (reverting to the title Chief Executive) in place by 1st September.

During this critical period, the Honorary Treasurer, Martin Evanson, who had been re-elected at the March AGM, had not attended any meetings of the management board since January, nor had any significant involvement in the federation's finances, and this came to a head at the May meeting when the board decided to ask him to resign, which he did.

Before leaving on the 31 March, Steve Gledhill had informed the management board that, in the absence of new income sources and drastic cost savings, the federation was heading for a loss of £1.2 million in the year to 30 September 1997; which would wipe out the reserves and result in an overall deficit of some £500,000. At this point the federation would be insolvent and unable to continue unless a recovery plan based on assured income sources were in place.

A poisoned chalice?

Some good news arrived when Ken Rickhuss was able to inform the Council on 7th June that the Sports Council, on behalf of the National Lottery, had agreed to fund coaching and athlete development to the extent of £2.5 million annually. However, because of the fears surrounding the BAF's financial situation, the Sports Council insisted that the funds be managed at arm's length from the federation's main business in order to protect them should the BAF get into real difficulties. Creating an acceptable structure to meet these conditions delayed the payment of funds and this further complicated the federation's cash flow problems.

The Officers, now including the new treasurer, Midlander Keith Atkins, who had been formally appointed at the Council meeting on 7th June, searched for ways out of their predicament but the inescapable fact was that the federation was running short of cash. The possibility of raising a loan and/or persuading Channel 4 to pay part of the rights fee for 1998 in advance came to nothing and an appeal to the AAA of England (with reserves of around £1.5 million) for help was refused.

But, amidst all this chaos, a search for another chief executive continued and, in July, David Moorcroft was appointed; to take up his position on 1st October 1997.

On 14th October 1997, two weeks after Moorcroft's appointment to the hot seat, the management board decided that it could not carry on and BAF was placed into administration.

Whether such a fateful step was actually necessary must be in doubt. Following the resignation of Steve Gledhill in January 1997 and the absences of Honorary Treasurer Evanson, Keith Atkins was probably brought on to the scene too late for him to fully get to grips with the complexities of the business and it is understandable that the snapshot of the financial situation he produced seemed to point in only one direction.

If it was true that the BAF had gone into deficit, the final decline was even more precipitous than generally portrayed. Only two years before, at the close of the financial year on 30 September 1995 (the last one for which I was responsible), the published reserves were £1,089,000 but this figure did not include a further approximately £1 million of "hidden reserves" as a result of the prudent accounting policies that had been adopted over a number of years. In addition, the British Athletic Foundation, which was in effect an arm of the BAF, had reserves of over £600,000 and which were available to shelter some of the BAF's

A poisoned chalice?

developmental costs if the BAF itself ran into difficulties. All told, there were therefore available reserves of over £2.5 million at the end of 1995.

No formal accounts were prepared for the BAF prior to its administration on 14th October 1997 and I do not know whether Management Accounts were produced during the final months or, if they were, whether they still exist. Nevertheless it is not difficult to calculate that, even after the loss of £640,000 in 1996, there should still have been actual reserves of around £1.9 million on 30 September 1996.

The statement of affairs produced by the administrators when they took office disclosed an overall deficit of £314,587 implying that the BAF had lost a staggering £2.2 million in the 12½ months since 30 September 1996. Admittedly, the administrators took a conservative view of the value of the federation's assets, writing down fixed assets by £100,000 to their "realisable value" and allowing for employees claims (only relevant if they were made redundant) of a further £100,000 and a "provision for further claims" (probably a guess) of £50,000. What appeared to be a catastrophic collapse in the federation's finances is hard to understand, especially when one considers that, on the day that it went into administration, the BAF's assets included around three quarters of a million pounds in the bank.

Little more than a year was to pass before UK Athletics was launched and which, in its first year, would generate a surplus of £210,000 on a turnover of over £7 million, including a healthy profit on promotions. In the meantime, the winding up of the federation was to drag on for almost 12 years before being finally concluded and the administrators' costs would amount to £499,000 with legal costs taking a further £426,000, a total of £925,000, with the inevitable result that the ordinary creditors, which included unpaid athletes, received only a fraction of their dues.

The Federation had clearly not taken the painful steps necessary to reduce costs in line with its reduced income and this was a serious failure of management. But it might still have survived if the cash flow situation could have been managed with, in particular, a new era of public funding through the Sport Council just around the corner.

Whether the survival of the BAF would have been in the interests of the sport is another matter as the shock of its bankruptcy effectively gave David Moorcroft, with the intervention and support of the Sports

A poisoned chalice?

Council, a chance to re-model the structure of the sport with a clean sheet that no previous administrators had enjoyed.

ATHLETIC AND TELEVISION

Athletics in Britain had been televised by the BBC since 1953 (at that time there was no alternative, of course) and viewers enjoyed some of the great moments during the 1950s and 1960s including the epic Chataway v Kuts race at the White City. ITV attempted to break this stranglehold unsuccessfully for year after year but had managed only to secure a domestic foothold with its broadcasting of the popular end of season meeting ("the Coke meet") promoted by the International Athletes' Club (IAC).

During the 1980s athletics was on a high after the record breaking and Olympic exploits of Coe, Ovett, Daley Thompson, Alan Wells, etc. and John Bromley, the charismatic head of ITV Sport, decided that ITV's time had come. The BBC contract was coming up for renewal and Bromley made his move in 1984 by making an offer that took the breath away; ITV would pay £10.5 million for the rights to broadcast British Athletics for five years from 1985 to 1990. Moreover, the contract could include a number of cross country and road running events (hitherto the Cinderellas of the sport) plus the British League club's final; plus the Welsh Games, Scottish Championships, Women's AAA championships, and the Northern Ireland Ulster Games; a total of 25 events annually.

The BBC made a competing offer that came close to ITV's but the sport opted for ITV and signed up.

ITV agreed a parallel contract with the IAC to cover three road races, one cross country and one track and field event and, having made it a condition that any other new athletic events had to be first offered to ITV, had the sport sewn up.

Had it been simply a choice between the two offers, the sport may well have opted to continue with the tried and tested BBC, even if the fees were slightly lower, but the ITV contract offered something that the BBC could not; advertising. The opportunities to offer greater value to sponsors (who, for example, could enhance their sponsorships by taking advertising in the commercial breaks during an athletics programme) that came with the ITV culture, and which also meant much higher sponsorship fees, could not be ignored and made the difference.

The ITV contract was shared with Channel 4 (where the head of sport was former Olympic athlete Adrian Metcalfe) and Bromley appointed Richard Russell as executive director of athletics with the remit to handle the day to day relationships with the sport. From the outset, Russell would attend meetings of the Joint Standing Committee which met quite frequently and this was supplemented by occasional "get to know you" dinners which Bromley and Metcalfe would attend.

This arrangement continued for the first year or so of the contract but gradually changed into more focused professional meetings, often including Alan Pascoe, as Andy Norman, Malcolm Jones and I assumed greater responsibility for the day to day management of the events and the contracts.

ITV had invested heavily in athletics and needed a commercial return and it should not be overlooked that the full cost to them was far more than the rights fees as athletics is one of the most complicated sports for television to broadcast effectively. ITV had, at least, to match the expertise and reputation for quality of the BBC and the costs of production were as much again as the rights fees.

If ITV could not justify the cost of its investment in athletics by the advertising revenue it could attract (this, in turn, depending crucially on the numbers of viewers), a renewal of the contract after five years would not be guaranteed. Would the BBC have welcomed athletics back with a generous offer in such circumstances?

Norman, Jones and I, if not many others in the sport, were acutely conscious of these imperatives and of the need to constantly achieve quality events in order to satisfy the paymasters. The relationship with Bromley and Russell was excellent and Bromley never took advantage of the powerful position over the sport that, in reality, he knew he had secured.

The key person in delivering the events was Andy Norman. It was his influence, above all, and his effective promotion of AAA events that created the climate that led ITV to lust after the athletics contract and it then fell to Andy Norman to deliver, time and again, the events that kept ITV interested. He did not suffer fools gladly and was feared and admired in equal measure. He had cultivated everyone of importance in world athletics from the IAAF President Primo Nebiolo down but, at the same time, sowed the seeds of his own eventual downfall.

Athletics and television

An important element in John Bromley's winning bid was that ITV would broadcast 25 events annually, provided that they were of sufficient quality. This element was something of an illusion as, in reality, many of the events were not likely to attract the viewing numbers that could justify their continued presence in a commercial broadcaster's schedule. And so it proved and the number of events actually broadcast dwindled so that, in the final year, only 17 were covered. It will also be recalled that, in the first months of the contract, cameras had been pulled from an event in Edinburgh because of unacceptable political advertising and, in the second year, an indoor event had not been screened because of poor quality.

The initial relationship with ITV had been bumpy but, nevertheless, personal relationships were good and, in early 1988, Richard Russell (pictured) made overtures for an extension of the contract beyond 1990. This time, ITV was seeking an arrangement to include the IAC in the joint contract and the IAC, through its chairman David Bedford, was agreeable to this. These discussions proceeded extremely amicably and speedily to a point where a very satisfactory contract extension could have been secured. However, the IAC suddenly withdrew from the negotiations and ITV shelved the deal. The reason given by the IAC was that *"with the future of one governing body unclear and the real possibility [existing] that [disagreement over] subventions* (payments to athletes)*.......may put us in direct conflict with the AAA"*.

This argument was hard to understand and probably had much to do with internal politics as it will be remembered that 1988 was the year of the "Southern Counties EGM" and David Bedford and Derek Johnson (together the leading forces in the IAC) had been heading the Southern campaign against the AAA and the McAllister plans for the BAF. Probably they thought that their positions would be compromised if they were seen to get into bed with the opposition but, whatever the reasons, a golden opportunity was passed up.

Richard Russell had offered a contract extension to 31 December 1992 which was the furthest he could go at that time as all the ITV franchises expired on that date and new bidders were jockeying for pieces

99

Athletics and television

of the ITV action. The future of the entire ITV system was in the melting pot, successful bidders would be expecting to recover their investments and budgets would come under close scrutiny. Viewing figures would become even more important and those programmes and sports that could not command good audiences would be under pressure. Athletics was one of the sports under scrutiny.

The climate for a possible renewal of the contract with ITV was, therefore, difficult and unpredictable and at a meeting in late 1988, Bromley announced that, in any renewal, ITV would be interested only in track and field events (perhaps 8 outdoor and 3 indoor events).

The opening shot in real contract discussions came in February 1989 when Bromley offered £3m for an extension to December 1992. This represented £1m per year for three summer seasons, less than half the previous contract. He also again made it clear that ITV was interested only in the cream, now defined as 7 outdoor and 3 indoor events, track and field only. They were not interested in cross country, road or the British League and the sport could do what it liked with those.

A year earlier, Richard Russell had offered £6.5m for a similar package of events.

The negotiations continued against such a background and, eventually, ITV was pushed to make an improved offer that included 8 outdoor and 3 indoor track and field events, the clubs' cup final, and one cross country and one road racing event. By now, ITV had decided that they could contract beyond the December 1992 watershed (the business had to go on and new franchise holders would have to accept existing commitments) and proposed £8m for a new four year contract.

Although this represented a small reduction on the £2.1m per year secured in 1985, with far fewer events to be funded it was a generous offer in the circumstances and owed much to John Bromley's personal integrity.

As the sport's negotiators, Andy, Malcolm and I were satisfied and relieved and waited for the formal rubber stamping by the ITV board.

Then came the bombshell; the ITV board said no.

This news was broken to the three of us by Bromley when he took us aside at the end of the first day's competition of the European Cup in Gateshead on 5 August 1989. This prestigious competition, bringing together the top eight European athletic nations, had never been won by Great Britain but there had been great excitement as Great Britain's men were leading their competition after the first day. As can be imagined, our elation at the success of the athletes was immediately shattered by this news.

Bromley, highly embarrassed, said that ITV now wanted only 6 outdoor events and no indoor competitions and could offer £5.5m for the rights to these events for four years.

Great Britain won in Gateshead, Linford Christie collected the trophy and suddenly athletics was in all the newspapers. Further negotiations culminated in a showdown at John Bromley's private dining club the Wig and Pen with Greg Dyke (chairman of the ITV sports group), Stuart McConachie (who had taken over from Richard Russell when the latter left to join Eurosport) and Bromley himself.

John Bromley (a legendary winer and diner) had been a member of the Wig and Pen Club for years and was a regular. Located on London's Strand opposite the Royal Courts of Justice, the Wig and Pen was a Dickensian establishment with narrow, twisting stairs that led to numerous private dining rooms. As the name implies, it was a haunt of lawyers and journalists.

Bromley had reserved one such room. The food was excellent but there was much at stake. Greg Dyke made it clear at the outset that he wanted to keep athletics on ITV but that he had to justify it. After a long lunch, the deal was finally done and ITV agreed to pay £7m for a four year contract to broadcast 6 outdoor events (5 of which would be on the important Friday night schedule) and 3 indoor events; and Channel 4 would cover the British League clubs cup final and maybe some other events. The contract details had to be worked out before the vital signatures would be added so there was still plenty of opportunity for a last minute hitch.

The deal that the three negotiators were so relieved to have won immediately ran into flak from within the sport, with accusations of selling out road and cross country and the Celtic regions. The Northern Irish Association complained that the Ulster Games was its financial lifeblood and the Southern Counties threatened to withdraw its Crystal Palace event from the deal as a gesture of solidarity with its allies.

Despite the need for confidentiality, details of the proposed deal soon leaked out. Les Jones, a member of the JSC and bound by its confidentiality, would admit that, in an attempt to salvage something for Northern Ireland, he had lobbied both the Southern Counties AA and his friend Brendan Foster, thinking that the latter could open a door to the BBC. David Bedford, at a JSC meeting on 10th October 1989, went so far as to accuse the negotiators of deliberately manipulating the discussions so as to exclude Northern Ireland, Cross Country and the IAC.

It looked as if the painfully won deal might unravel and the public bickering was extremely dangerous as the sport risked ITV changing its mind and walking away. Had this happened the sport would have been left swinging in the wind as the likelihood of a rival offer from the BBC was remote and the malcontents would have had to accept a heavy responsibility. Fortunately, wiser heads prevailed and the proposed contract was accepted at a joint meeting of the AAA General Committee and the BAAB Council on 21 October 1989 after a long explanation of the negotiations by Andy Norman and me.

Approaches to Channel 4 to take some of the events rejected by ITV did, however, prove successful and Channel 4 agreed to cover the UK Championships and the Belfast Games.

ITV had negotiated separately with the IAC and reached a parallel agreement.

Television income had thus been secured until March 1994 and these were to be John Bromley's parting gifts to athletics as he resigned from ITV soon after.

But the seas ahead would remain rough.

THE END OF A BEAUTIFUL FRIENDSHIP?

The world of ITV was changing. John Bromley had worked in television for 25 years and had been head of ITV sport since 1981 and his place was taken by Bob Burrows, also steeped in TV sport but who was to find life uncomfortable in the new culture. Paul Fox, a former well known figure in the BBC, commenting in the *Daily Telegraph*, offered advice to Rugby that applied equally to all sports. Remarking that Bob Burrows and his colleagues were honourable men, he underlined that a contract would not be with them but *"with those faceless schedulers in Grays Inn Road* (the location of ITV's offices) *whose priorities are different from those who have sport's interests at heart"*. Key amongst these was Marcus Plantin, Director of Programmes.

Andy Norman, Malcolm Jones and I, who had been regularly meeting TV and marketing contacts, were already picking up these vibes and realised that we had to rethink strategy. We needed to bring the BBC back to the table and to investigate other potential partners such as the emerging satellite broadcaster Sky Television.

We had also realised that the BAF's package of events had remained substantially unchanged for too long and that new ideas were needed.

When John Bromley resigned from ITV in late 1989, he had joined former BBC producers Mike Murphy and Brian Venner as chairman of Television Sport and Leisure Limited (TSL) a production company and television consultancy based in London. Bromley knew the TV sports scene better than most and could see clearly the problems that lay ahead. He wanted to maintain a business relationship with British athletics and kept in touch.

The BAF itself was searching for ways to strengthen its hand in its dealings with television but knew that, to have a good chance of success, it needed to boost its programme of events, either in number or quality or both.

The leading European international meetings were the Weltklasse (Zurich), Memorial Van Damme (Brussels), Bislett Games (Oslo) and Istaf (Berlin) and they had been co-operating in marketing under the banner "Golden Four". Through his contacts with the organisers of each of these meetings, Andy Norman had persuaded them that an expansion of the series to include the London Grand Prix would make commercial sense.

To the outside world, Great Britain had what was regarded as one of the most successful commercial packages of televised athletic events anywhere and was in a position to be envied. The attractions to the *Four* of joining such a package were considerable and a series of highly secret meetings was started. These usually took place at a London airport hotel with Wilfried Meert (Brussels), Svein Arne Hansen (Oslo) and Andreas Brugger (Zurich) flying in to join Andy Norman, Malcolm Jones and me; and Bromley and Murphy from TSL.

Bit by bit, during the first half of 1992, a deal was worked out to expand the four into a five by adding London, but with the added ingredient that the BAF, as a strong federation, would guarantee and manage the television and marketing rights of all five. Effectively, the BAF would be adding to its portfolio the rights to the five most important athletic invitation meetings in the world. This would have given it considerable clout in dealing with television broadcasters and sponsors.

Bromley and Murphy were essential partners as, through TSL, they had undertaken to procure and guarantee the worldwide television coverage without which there could be no deal.

These negotiations proceeded very amicably and, by June 1992, all the main conditions were agreed in principle and draft legal contracts were prepared. Everything depended on the delivery of television coverage and income but TSL was finding this more difficult than they had so confidently predicted. In the meantime, the German UFA TV organisation was bidding heavily for the rights to the Golden Four and, to the disappointment of the BAF and TSL, the Zurich event decided to accept its offer and the other three followed suit.

In the meantime, relationships with ITV were going downhill. The value of athletics within ITV was being questioned and Bob Burrows and Stuart McConachie were in despair. The BBC, although showing interest in the AAA Championships/Trials, was not yet ready to take over the whole contract, Sky and Channel 4 were interested but had no budget and this left ITV as the only remaining player, however unpalatable.

The waning interest by commercial television was a consequence of a steady drift downwards in viewing figures. In the first few years of the

The end of a beautiful friendship?

ITV contract, it was quite common to see viewing figures of 7 million or more. Indeed, the Peugeot Talbot Games held at Crystal Palace stadium in 1985 generated 8.5m on the first day and a massive 11m on the second of the two day event. An indoor event typically generated 3 or 4m viewers. The weaker events were quickly exposed, however, and, in 1986, the Scottish Championships were broadcast only in Scotland and watched by a mere 0.3m. Likewise, road races were not producing consistently good figures. On the whole, however, ITV was satisfied with the statistics in the early years of the contract.

By 1991 the figures were sliding. The flagship London Grand Prix (now called the TSB Grand Prix, a new sponsor having replaced Peugeot) generated 7.5m viewers for the first hour on ITV and 4.55m on Channel 4 for the second hour. In 1992, the figures drifted to 6.7m and 4.4m respectively and the declining viewing figures became a topic of debate at every meeting between the sport's representatives and ITV.

It needs to be realised that ITV Sport was fighting an internal battle to maintain airtime against populist programmes such as Coronation Street, The Bill and others; programmes that, in those days, regularly attracted viewing figures in excess of 16 or even 20 million. It was accepted that most sports could not hope to compete and win against such opposition and ITV had a statutory duty to produce a balanced schedule of programmes. Nevertheless, as a commercial operation, the programme planners of ITV could hardly be expected to smile benignly on a sport that, as they saw it, was too expensive to justify and was occupying prime time slots at the most popular viewing times. Viewing figures directly affected advertising income so the most popular programmes should logically occupy the most popular viewing times.

And this was all against a background where the ITV franchises had expired at the end of 1992 and the Thatcher Government had decided to put the new franchises to auction. Thus, most of the new franchise holders had paid heavily to secure their rights and needed to maximise revenue to warrant their investments.

Where could athletics fit into this?

What quickly became clear was that, with John Bromley's influence gone, athletics would have to justify itself commercially to the new regime and the first meeting with new Chief Executive Andrew Quinn made this brutally clear when the sport was informed that athletic events would be downgraded to a thirty minute slot only. Up until this time, the

The end of a beautiful friendship?

track and field events had enjoyed a whole hour live on ITV followed by a further hour live on Channel 4. A downgrade to only a half hour would not only drastically reduce the exposure of the sport but would decimate potential income from sponsors.

The second, hard won, contract with ITV would run out in March 1994 so, if the sport was to have any hope of a further renewal on decent terms, and with time running out, the 1993 season would be crucial and something special was needed if anything was to be salvaged.

The something special was devised by Andy Norman; a head to head contest between the two most famous sprinters in the world, Carl Lewis and Linford Christie. Lewis was the world record holder and Christie, the reigning Olympic Champion from 1992 in Barcelona, the hottest property in British athletics. Norman had been credited with guiding Christie's career to the Olympic title and was the only man who could pull off such a clash.

Norman had done his homework and, having convinced Malcolm Jones and me that the clash could be self financing, went ahead with our support. The venue was Gateshead during the Vauxhall Motors sponsored meeting on Friday evening, 30th July, and attracted massive media interest. It seemed that every newspaper in Britain devoted column after column to the showdown, the stadium sold out and ITV, which had contributed most of the budget, was rewarded with unprecedented viewing figures of 12m. Linford Christie beat Carl Lewis to satisfy the fans and went on a couple of weeks later to take the gold medal at the World championships in Stuttgart.

ITV was delighted with the event but would it be enough to clinch a new deal? It seemed so, as contract negotiations moved more smoothly and, by early October, the outline of a new four year contract was agreed with Bob Burrows and Trevor East; ITV would take 4 outdoor invitation meetings per year and would pay £7m rights fee. The AAA Championships could be sold to the BBC and, all in all, it was a good result in the circumstances, albeit a far cry from the heady days of the first contract.

On 25 October, however, I received a phone call at home at 7pm from a crestfallen Bob Burrows to say that the ITV board had decided that they were not interested in athletics and that the whole deal was off. No explanation was forthcoming.

The end of a beautiful friendship?

By coincidence, I was to be in London at a BAF meeting the following day and agreed to call in to see Burrows and East after the meeting. This I did and, at 6.30pm, found a dispirited Burrows and East with little to offer except a consoling glass or two and mutual commiserations. After half an hour or so of desultory conversation, I asked if Director of Programmes Marcus Plantin was still there and, if so, could I see him. Plantin joined the group and defended the decision on cost grounds. I complained that athletics had been treated badly after reaching a good faith understanding with Burrows and East and demanded a formal meeting with Andrew Quinn, the Chief Executive.

I had argued that to pull the plug on athletics in such a brutal fashion after a nine year relationship would be as damaging to ITV's reputation as to athletics'. Admittedly, this was something of a bluff but it did the trick and, following some tense meetings with Quinn, a stay of execution was negotiated: ITV would continue until the end of 1994, thus giving athletics time to make new arrangements for the future - if it could.

Inevitably, news of the spat crept into the open and John Bromley, in one of his occasional articles in the *Daily Telegraph*, described it thus:

"On hearing this news (the pulling of the plug), *Lister and Norman marched on the ITV Centre in London's Grays Inn Road. ITV's two top programme bosses, Andrew Quinn and Marcus Plantin, found themselves in a fierce argument, with the aggressive Norman in full flow. The word "trust" was used on several occasions.*

"The result of that angry exchange is that the ITV bosses had a rethink and will come back with an offer to extend the present contract by just one year, with a fee of around £1 million for the four domestic events.

"Norman and Lister will then have to judge this scenario: take an unsatisfactory one-year deal with ITV which would deliver four peak time slots - and thus excite the sponsors - or go walk-about again and attempt to persuade Channel Four or the BBC to give them a four year deal with not so much money but a secure future."

In reality, the sport had no choice as we had already talked to both the BBC and Channel Four as well as the fledgling Sky and knew that a comprehensive deal with either broadcaster was not an option at that point in time. BBC had offered a three year deal to cover the AAA championships but it was too soon for them to go further. The obvious

The end of a beautiful friendship?

course was to accept the ITV deal and then to try to repair relationships while, at the same time, building a new relationship with the BBC with an eye to the longer term.

There was no time to lose as the ITV stay of execution would rapidly come to an end and the BAF needed urgently to secure its future as, without the vital income from TV and sponsorship, the whole organisation would be in peril.

This was a very tense time for the BAF and, at the very time that some stability was needed, potential disaster had struck.

As we have seen, Malcolm Jones had resigned as chief executive in April 1993 and Peter Radford, who had been appointed executive chairman in November 1993, had terminated Andy Norman's employment on 29 April 1994. Ian Stewart, one of Britain's most successful middle distance runners and who had been Norman's assistant, took over as Director of Promotions but was an unknown entity to ITV.

What to do?

It seemed that it was still too soon to interest the BBC in taking on the full athletics contract and that the likelihood of securing an acceptable financial deal from the BBC would be even remoter if it was known that the ITV relationship was at an end.

In such inauspicious circumstances, it was decided to go for broke and to make a new pitch to ITV at Andrew Quinn and Marcus Plantin levels. A sophisticated formal presentation of athletics was devised and presented by Peter Radford, Ian Stewart and me on 12 May 1994.

When we had arrived at the ITV Centre in Grays Inn Road to make our pitch we were greeted with the news that Labour Party Leader John Smith had died and all the news programmes were focusing on this national event. It meant that our presentation would be delayed and that Marcus Plantin (who we had felt was, to say the least, cool towards athletics and needed to be convinced) would not be available. However, Andrew Quinn, the chief executive, and Bob Burrows did listen to us and the presentation seemed to have been well received; but, were they merely being polite or had the door been reopened?

Further meetings were held and deadlines came and went. The prospects of a successful outcome looked gloomy and, after a further

The end of a beautiful friendship?

meeting with ITV on 26 July, Ian Stewart and I thought that we were too far apart on price. Obviously we had played a better hand than we thought as a phone call from Trevor East, Bob Burrows' assistant, two days later brought news of an offer. ITV had agreed to the requested price and the result was that the one year arrangement with ITV was extended by two years to the end of 1996 with an option for a further two years, the option to be decided by the end of 1995. ITV would pay £1.4m per year for the extra two years.

This deal included a twist that had been in the background for years but had hitherto been sidelined; programme sponsorship. This concept was a potential money spinner for ITV who, under new rules, could sell the opportunity for a company to be the "sponsor of a programme". Such a company would feature at the beginning and end of a programme and at the beginning and end of each advertising break; and this is now common but was then untried. This was potentially disastrous for sport which relied on sponsors who in turn expected their advertising boards to be seen prominently during the broadcast of the events they were sponsoring and would not expect their competitors to share this exposure.

These sponsors had brought substantial monies into athletics, money which was now at risk. To understand the problem, imagine that, say, Peugeot Motors has paid handsomely to be the title sponsor of "the Peugeot Games" only to discover that the television transmission is to be "presented by", say, Ford Motors. The potential for conflicts of this kind was obvious. The BAF and their sponsorship selling agents, APA, were desperate to avoid such clashes but ITV was equally determined to exploit this new income source and the negotiations over this right that ITV demanded were tense. Eventually, in order to protect its sponsor income, the BAF agreed to effectively buy out the programme sponsorship rights and endeavour to sell them on to its own sponsors.

Against the odds, therefore, athletics had secured what were, in the circumstances, acceptable TV contracts. This would extend the relationship with ITV to 12 years but each contract renewal had been fraught and the BAF needed to plan on the basis that it would not go on.

An attempt had been made to interest the BBC when the first ITV contract came up for renewal but this had been too soon as the BBC was still sore at losing out in 1985. But relationships had been maintained with Head of Sport Jonathan Martin and his deputy John Rowlinson and, by early 1993, the BBC had been ready to talk again. As it became clearer that any new contract with ITV would probably be even more restrictive than before,

The end of a beautiful friendship?

the possibility of parallel arrangements with the BBC emerged. The BBC had continued to be the broadcaster of choice of major international events such as the Olympic Games, World and European championships and Commonwealth Games and, as a logical extension of these into the domestic programme, might be willing to contract the AAA Championships, which doubled as trials for the major events, indoors and outdoors.

This proved to be the case and the BBC contracted to cover the AAA Championships/Trials, both indoors and outdoors, for £660,000 over the three years 1994, 1995, 1996.

Planning for and negotiations with television were treadmills from which it was impossible to escape (and certainly never relax) and no sooner had the deal with ITV been put to bed than it was necessary to worry once again about the future. With contracts with both ITV and the BBC due to expire at the end of 1996 and ITV not expected to take up its option (deadline 31 December 1995), some new strategic thinking was needed.

Relationships with ITV reached a new low in 1996 when, after losing a ratings battle with the BBC over the European football championships, the programme controllers became disenchanted with sport. A scheduled BAF event at Crystal Palace was dropped in favour of a "soap" and the expected coverage of a subsequent event in Gateshead was drastically reduced. Although ITV paid their rights fee for these events in full, as they were contractually obliged to do, the loss of airtime resulted in sponsors claiming their money back.

As expected, ITV decided not to exercise its option for the additional two years and the BAF, back on the treadmill, turned to Channel 4 where Mike Millar was the head of sport. Channel 4 had, of course been a junior partner with ITV in all the athletics contracts since 1985 so were familiar with the subject.

Geoff Parsons and Roger Black, representing the fledgling British Athletes Association, also agreed to attend presentation meetings with broadcasters to give the assurance that athletes would back any deal with their attendances at the events and it was probably this factor that swung discussions that had been opened with Channel 4 and led to an offer of a four year contract covering 1997 to 2000.

In the words of Mike Miller, Channel 4's head of sport,

The end of a beautiful friendship?

"*I would say the fact that the British Athletes Association was so enthusiastic about helping to find new ways to bring athletics up to date..........and to become intimately involved with both the events and the TV production processes, helped clinch the deal.*"

However, even before the first year of the contract with Channel 4 had ended, the BAF went into administration and the balance of the contract was taken up by the new UK Athletics. Subsequently, in a further twist of fate, Mike Millar was appointed head of sport at the BBC on Jonathan Martin's retirement and, when the Channel 4 deal expired, took athletics back to the BBC.

It was perhaps remarkable that the BAF (and, before it, the AAA-BAAB), managed to cling on to its lifeblood income from television for so long. The lucrative deal with ITV in 1985 was never likely to be repeated; John Bromley had shrewdly enticed the sport with money and promises of a breadth of exposure that was unsustainable on commercial TV where ratings were, and are, everything. Except for the few big track events, athletics could not survive in such an environment. Having burned its boats with the BBC, athletics ended up with nowhere else to go and could count itself lucky that, because of the basic decency of Bromley, Burrows and East, ITV did not exploit this as it could have.

Somehow, the sport struggled on, from one contract to another, slipping from the comfortable arms of the BBC, firstly to ITV and then to Channel 4. Probably, it should never have left the BBC in the first place but was seduced by a mixture of greed, inexperience, naivety and a lack of strategic forward thinking. At the time of writing, athletics is back with the BBC and the sport is under an entirely new form of management.

ANDY NORMAN

Andy Norman, in his youth, was a good club standard athlete, with best times of 49.8 for 440 yards and 1:54.1 for 800m. He became a policeman, rising to the rank of sergeant in the Metropolitan Police in London, but retained his interest in athletics and became involved in the Met Police Athletic Club and the Southern Counties Association. He quickly made a name for himself as someone who could get things done and became more and more involved in the organisation of events which, in turn, led him into contact with the athletes.

In the 1970s most of the important competitions were in Europe where events in Zurich, Oslo and elsewhere were attracting attention. These events commanded large budgets, provided by TV and sponsors, but needed a flow of top class athletes to satisfy their paymasters' demands for quality competition.

British stars and others were much in demand and Andy Norman gained the confidence of many of Britain's top athletes, including in particular middle distance record breaker Steve Ovett, and seized the opportunity with the contacts he had made to feed these athletes into the European events. This was good for these athletes, of course, but where Norman was clever was that he made it a condition that, along with the stars, the European meeting promoters also had to take up and coming athletes who needed the competition. This approach made everyone happy and provided valuable international experience for a wide range of British athletes. Thus Andy Norman created a reputation for himself.

The two most innovative events staged in Britain in the early eighties were the Peugeot Games, organised by the Southern Counties Association in midsummer and the end of season Coke (Coca Cola) event organised by the International Athletes Club. The key to these events was the quality of the athletes and it was essential to attract the best. Andy

Norman was the person who provided this and he became the crucial person in both events. His role in the IAC event was eventually taken over by David Bedford but Norman continued in his role with the Southern event as it was absorbed into the sport's mainstream package of commercial events.

Norman's influence and importance within athletics grew steadily and he became immersed in the organisation of international events in Britain. In 1987, towards the end of his illustrious running career, Sebastian Coe described Andy Norman thus. "*We owe a great deal to Andy*", he said. "*The greatest thing he ever did was to get British athletes into the right competitive environment by bringing top class athletes into this country*".

Andy Norman was the key figure in the negotiations which led to ITV outbidding the BBC for the British athletics contract in 1984. ITV's John Bromley had also made it clear that he (Norman) should be contracted by the sport as the organiser of the events in order to guarantee the delivery of what ITV had paid for. He therefore resigned from the Police Force and became the Promotions Officer under a contract with the AAA and BAAB.

Naively, the AAA-BAAB agreed to contract Norman as a "consultant" and not as an employee. This meant that, although being contracted for only 42 weeks per annum, he was paid what was effectively a full time employee's salary and was also free to pursue other activities; with some practical restraints admittedly. He was forbidden to work for the BBC, ITV or Channel 4 but no mention was made of Eurosport for whom he subsequently did athletics commentary and which attracted criticism, but was something the AAA-BAAB could not stop.

Whereas his importance and influence within the sport were growing, his reputation and relationships were more controversial. Amongst athletes, he was held in a mixture of awe and fear. For those whom he favoured there was almost no limit to their possibilities to gain access to important and lucrative competitions but for those who would not toe the Norman line, most doors were closed.

His relationships with colleagues and others who were at a senior level or who were important commercially were usually excellent and those who saw him at work in a crucial negotiation or presentation, as I did frequently, were invariably impressed by his knowledge and professionalism. But those whom he regarded as inferior he could treat appallingly and there were several occasions when he brought junior staff to tears.

The sporting press found Norman particularly offensive and had to put up with frequent invective and abuse, without being able to retaliate as they needed him as a vital source of athletic intelligence of all kinds. They were to take their opportunity for revenge over the tragic suicide of Cliff Temple.

Despite his hard man image as a bruiser, Andy Norman could also be exceptionally kind and soft hearted. He undoubtedly loved his sport and was determined to do everything he could to promote its development. His travelling was prodigious and much of this was spent visiting athletic clubs up and down the country. Frequently, he would delve into the boot of his car and bring out a Great Britain tracksuit or vest or some other item that he would give to the club he had visited for them to use in a raffle or other fund raising event.

His relationship with Fatima Whitbread drew accusations of favouring her with over-generous competition appearance fees at the expense of her rival, former Olympic Champion Tessa Sanderson. His relationship with Whitbread and his subsequent divorce from his Norwegian first wife soured relationships with Steve Ovett and his wife (Norman had been the best man at their wedding) but his marriage to Whitbread also eventually foundered.

Controversy was never far from Andy Norman.

In July 1989 £25,000 in cash was stolen from his hotel room prior to a grand prix event at Crystal Palace.

It has to be said that, in those days, it was common that athletes' appearance monies were paid in cash and huge sums of money changed hands in hotel rooms across Europe, so the fact that Norman was handling such money (in fact, £25,000 was by no means the whole budget) was not unusual. British athletes competing in Britain were not paid in cash (their earnings were transferred directly into their trust funds) but it was the norm for foreign athletes.

The police were informed but their enquiries led to nothing.

A month later, another scandal broke out.

In 1989, Sebastian Coe's and Steve Ovett's glory days were behind them but, apart from major championships, the head to head clash that the sporting public had longed for had not materialised. At last, if a little late, the clash was to take place at the AAA Championships which doubled as the trial for the Commonwealth Games, scheduled for New Zealand the following January.

On the day of the race a storm broke when Ovett said he would not run in the final of the 1500m. To everyone's mystification, Steve Ovett gave an emotional interview to ITV, saying that he was upset because he had been offered money to run and Seb Coe had not. The villain of the piece who had allegedly offered the money was, of course, Andy Norman.

ITV, the broadcasters, had built up their advance publicity on this clash and could see a disaster looming. No one could understand why Ovett should complain about being paid (the amount was said to be £20,000) – they could understand if others were paid and he was not - and the official rule was that no one was paid to compete in the AAA Championships.

In the event, Ovett was persuaded to run and was easily beaten by Coe.

The controversy raged in the national press and at its meeting on 18th August 1988, the AAA's F&GP Committee decided on an independent enquiry into Steve Ovett's allegations against Andy Norman. David Pickup (chief executive of the Sport Council) and Peter Reid QC agreed to conduct the enquiry but they were unable to find enough evidence to reach a clear verdict. They did, however, recommend strongly that clearer procedures should be put in place for the control of Norman's activities.

For a time, matters seemed to settle down but, below the surface, other controversies were simmering.

When Malcolm Jones became Chief Executive in December 1991, one of his priorities was to provide stronger management over Andy Norman and, once and for all, to end the unsatisfactory consultancy arrangement and put him on a proper employment contract. Realising that this was an "offer he should not refuse", Norman agreed to the change and a contract of employment was prepared by the BAF's solicitors. Before signing off the contract, Norman was forced by the BAF to confront his own reputation and other allegations about him; the BAF insisted on, and got, his absolute undertaking to "mend his ways", or else!

But Norman could not escape his own reputation and, in July 1992, the BBC broadcast a programme in its "On the Line" series which attacked his role in athletics. Suggestions were made of complicity in the avoidance of doping tests and conflicts of interest. The programme was full of innuendo but no hard facts and, despite lodging a strong complaint with the BBC, there was little that the sport or Norman could do.

During 1993, a respected and popular athletics journalist, Cliff Temple, was preparing an article for the *Sunday Times* which was expected to be critical of Norman. Norman had got wind of this and had telephoned Temple to "warn him off" but the article duly appeared on 1st August 1993.

In January 1994, Temple, who had been suffering from depression following his divorce, committed suicide and Norman was accused of contributing to his death by making false accusations about his (Temple's) relationship with one of the female athletes he coached. The conclusions of the subsequent inquest did not go that far but the fatal damage to Norman's reputation had been done and the press went to town on him, seeing this as their long awaited chance to repay the abuse they had borne over so many years.

The BAF acted and chairman Peter Radford suspended Norman pending an investigation.

Andy Norman was not without his sympathisers, however, and, in a letter to *Athletics Weekly*, respected middle distance coach Frank Horwill wrote, *"How sad that his (Temple's) life's work will most probably be remembered for a sordid dispute and the tragic method of his death. How ironic that his death is to be used as a lever to dethrone another world famous figure in athletics (Norman)."*

On 8 April 1994, Radford announced in a Press Release that *"I have concluded that Mr Norman's conduct in certain matters was not appropriate for someone employed as Director of Promotions of BAF and that it would be inconsistent with the interests of BAF for Mr Norman to remain in our employment".*

Radford went on to emphasise that it had been no part of his function to enquire into the causes or circumstances of the death of the late Cliff Temple. He also mentioned the positive contribution made to British athletics by Norman and hoped that *"in future a more balanced view of Andy Norman's contribution.....will emerge in the media than has sometimes been the case recently".*

Andy Norman

In truth, Radford and the BAF were in an impossible position. Whether or not there had been any substance to the allegations made against Andy Norman, he paid the price for years of treating the athletics writers with barely concealed contempt and they seized the chance of hitting back. Had the BAF decided to support Norman and continue his employment, the vendetta against Norman would have continued unabated and could have wreaked untold damage on what was already a weakened sport. Radford, supported by the BAF, took the pragmatic decision to part company with Norman.

History will probably judge Andy Norman an enigma. His contribution to British athletics up to the time of his sacking was undoubtedly immense. Almost single handedly, he dragged athletics into the modern era and a generation of British athletic stars credit him with the opportunities they had and the skill with which he guided their careers. But there is an equal number who believe he did as much damage to the sport's reputation. The financial bonanza of the roughly 10 years from 1985 owes much to his skill in putting together international athletic events in Britain that were the envy of the world.

His steamrolling character had much in common with that of IAAF President Primo Nebiolo, an egocentric who was admired and scorned in equal measure but who led the IAAF from relative obscurity to become a world power in international sport.

Although he was an essential part of the hierarchy of British athletics, most found Norman difficult to deal with and almost impossible to manage. In all honesty, he was probably unmanageable and therein lay the seeds of his destruction.

The story of Andy Norman is essentially a tragedy.

It fell to Ian Stewart, Norman's deputy, to pick up the pieces.

WHAT ABOUT THE ATHLETES?

In 1976, Great Britain had returned from the Olympic Games in Montreal with only one medal, the bronze in the 10,000m won by Brendan Foster. This was to prove a low point that marked the beginning of a period of astonishing success for British athletes.

By the time of the 1980 Games, held in Moscow, British athletes were already riding high. Steve Ovett and Sebastian Coe had started swapping middle distance world records and Daley Thompson had established himself as king of the decathlon. In Moscow, Coe was the favourite for the 800m but won the 1500m and Ovett was the favourite for the 1500m but won the 800m. Allan Wells took the 100m gold as well as silver in the 200m and Daley Thompson won the decathlon. The USA had led a partial boycott of these games which undoubtedly helped Britain's chances but did not take the gloss off the successes

The roll had begun.

British athletes were dominating the international stage, with superstars Coe, Ovett and Thompson joined by David Moorcroft, Fatima Whitbread, Tessa Sanderson and others. Coe and Ovett continued on their world record breaking roller coaster, including Coe's brilliant 800m record set in Florence in 1981. In 1982, David Moorcroft set a new world record for the 5,000m and Steve Cram emerged as European Champion over 1,500m. Daley Thompson continued on his winning ways and triple jumper Keith Connor also took European Gold.

1981 also signified a further milestone in the sport in Britain with the first running of the London Marathon. Chris Brasher had been inspired by the New York marathon to organise one in London and, against the odds, had persuaded all the necessary authorities to support him. Today, the London Marathon is as much a part of London life and tradition as the Changing of the Guard.

Brasher, irascible but immensely likeable, was another larger than life character who, when he set his mind to something, could get it done. He had taken part as one of the pace-makers in Roger Bannister's four minute mile and had won the steeplechase gold medal at the 1956 Olympic Games in Melbourne. Mountain climbing and walking were hobbies (he had been a reserve on Sir John Hunt's successful team to be the first to

What about the athletes?

conquer Everest) and together with London Marathon co-founder John Disley, he promoted orienteering as a serious sport.

For a few years I was a director of the London Marathon and I recall an occasion when I had arranged to meet Chris Brasher after one of the day's programme of events at the Commonwealth Games in New Zealand in 1992 to discuss some Marathon business. We had agreed to go for dinner directly from the stadium and Chris turned up straight from the press seats looking rather dishevelled after a day's work. Arriving at the restaurant he remarked that "this looks rather posh, I had better make myself more presentable"; with which he delved into the boot of his hire car, emerged with a large spotted handkerchief, knotted it around his neck and announced that he was ready.

By the beginning of the eighties, money, if not yet paid "over the counter" was freely available to the top performers who, increasingly, competed where the money was. As a consequence, it became harder and harder to persuade Britain's stars to turn out in the domestic events; events which generated the cash needed to run the sport. Things came to a head in 1982.

The BAAB's report on the season complained that "*all too often our top athletes find other priorities than supporting the BAAB and British athletics*". Conscious of the need to provide spectators and television with quality athletics, the BAAB issued a "*run or don't go to Athens (venue of the European Championships)*" ultimatum. This had the desired effect of producing an outstanding August Bank Holiday Games at Crystal Palace stadium but soured relationships with the athletes, a problem that continued to simmer and which would return to haunt the British Athletic Federation.

Later in 1982, a landmark was passed when the IAAF decided to officially recognise payments to athletes and inaugurated the trust fund system.

The period of outstanding success by Britain's athletes after 1980 had created the conditions for ITV's successful bid for British athletics' broadcasting rights and this, in turn, provided the money to ensure that these great athletes would be seen competing in Britain.

Also during this period, administrators had begun their long and tortuous journey towards the British Athletic Federation and these often acrimonious negotiations frequently burst into public with potentially

What about the athletes?

damaging effects on the reputation of the sport. Fortunately, the "corridors of power" rarely appeared to affect the endeavours of the athletes, probably because most of them and their coaches felt that they prospered in spite of the official systems.

The BAF was supposed to change everything for the better, so the administrators persevered.

The first ever world championships in athletics were held in Helsinki in 1983 and witnessed the drama of Britain's Fatima Whitbread leading the final of the javelin competition until local heroine Tiina Lillak snatched the gold with her very last throw. Daley Thompson again beat his great rival, the German Jurgen Hingsen, in the decathlon and Steve Cram took the 1500m.

With another Olympic Games, that in Los Angeles in 1984, on the horizon, excitement with British athletics had reached fever pitch with the arrival in Britain of the running phenomenon, South African Zola Budd. The bare footed runner had received a British passport in record time and thus was eligible to compete for Great Britain in the Olympics, South Africa remaining excluded from international sport because of its apartheid policies.

The Olympic clash between Budd and the USA's record breaker Mary Decker ended with Decker's fall during the race, having apparently been tripped by Budd, and Budd herself finished seventh. Britain's Wendy Sly finished second but her silver medal success was overshadowed by the Budd/Decker controversy.

The 1984 Olympics saw Daley Thompson retain his decathlon crown and Sebastian Coe brilliantly retained his 1500m title, the only athlete to do so, and once again took silver in the 800m. Steve Cram took the silver medal in the 1500m behind Coe and Tessa Sanderson won the javelin. In addition, David Ottley won silver in the men's javelin, Fatima Whitbread bronze in the women's javelin, Shirley Strong took a silver in the women's 100m hurdles and Kathy Cook bronze in the women's 400m. All in all, it was a highly successful Games for Great Britain's athletes.

As 1984 turned into 1985 Steve Cram emerged as the new king of the middle distance, setting three world records in as many weeks over 1500m, the mile and 2000m. The European Junior championships of the same year saw British athletes harvest 18 medals including 10 gold. The

What about the athletes?

new generation, that included Colin Jackson, Roger Black, John Regis and Jon Ridgeon, had arrived with perfect timing.

The old guard had not quite finished and gave a farewell flourish at the 1986 European Championships in Stuttgart. Seb Coe, who had never won a major title over the distance at which he held the world record, finally succeeded, leading a clean sweep of medals in the 800m and taking the gold ahead of Tom McKean and Steve Cram. The roles were reversed in the 1500m when Cram just held off a fast finishing Coe to take the gold.

Elsewhere, Fatima Whitbread had set the stadium alight with a world record in the qualifying round of the women's javelin and maintained her form to win the gold in the final, ahead of her nemesis Lillak and deposed world record holder Petra Felke from East Germany. Linford Christie (100m), Roger Black (400m) and Daley Thompson (decathlon) each added European gold to the Commonwealth titles they had gained earlier in the year in Edinburgh and Jack Buckner became European Champion over 5000m. Steve Ovett, in a last hurrah, had won the 5000m at the Commonwealth Games.

The main events in 1987 were the European Cup in Prague, to be followed by the second world championships in Rome.

Britain had never won the European Cup and the men's team finished a respectable third, with the women fifth.

The world championships in Rome saw Britain produce a solid if unspectacular performance with only one gold medal, from Fatima Whitbread in the women's javelin. Linford Christie had become involved in a dispute with head coach Frank Dick over the running order in the sprint relay and this escalated into a public and much publicised altercation with the press. Although he claimed that his running had not been affected, Christie could manage only fourth in the 100m.

British pride was recovered with a typically gutsy run by Peter Elliott to take the 800m silver medal; Jon Ridgeon and Colin Jackson took silver and bronze respectively in the 110m hurdles; John Regis took silver in the 200m; Jack Buckner took bronze in the 5000m; and the 4x400m relay team took silver. This championship saw the end of a legend when Daley Thompson finally ran out of fitness and years and finished out of the medals. As a mark of their respect for him the decathlon medallists insisted that Daley accompany them on their lap of honour.

What about the athletes?

1988 meant another Olympic Games, this time in Seoul, South Korea but, back at home, the BAF was still only a dream.

For the 1988 Games the BAAB had adopted a new selection policy; the first two in the official trials would be selected automatically provided they had achieved the designated qualification standard. The third place (only 3 entrants are allowed) would be decided by the selectors.

Seb Coe was anxious for a final shot at the Olympic 800m but finished outside the first two at the trials. Cram, who had run and qualified for the 800m, did not run in the 1500m but had declared a wish to double up. Likewise, Peter Elliott had won the 1500m trial but wanted to run the 800m as well. The quandary for the selectors was whether to pick Elliott or Coe for the third spot in the 800m. The selectors opted for Coe; but there was a twist. In those days, the selectors' responsibility was merely to recommend selections to the BAAB Council, which had the final word, and this would lead to the farce of the Council effectively going over, event by event, the same ground that had already been debated by the selectors. Most selections were not controversial but there were usually a few where, sometimes, an individual Council member blatantly argued for the inclusion of an athlete from his or her region.

The BAAB Council overturned the selectors and picked Elliott for the 800m and all hell broke loose, with the press having a field day. The *Daily Mirror* ran a "Coe Must Go" campaign and the President of the IOC, Samaranch, an admirer of Coe, floated the idea of a "wild card" entry but, in the end, Sebastian Coe did not get his wish.

The 1988 Olympic Games in Seoul acquired notoriety because of the Ben Johnson doping scandal but also witnessed the emergence of Linford Christie as a world class sprinter. Christie, himself surviving a brush with the anti-doping regime in Seoul, became the first European to run the 100m in less than 10 seconds and was elevated to the silver medal position behind American legend Carl Lewis when Johnson was disqualified.

Elsewhere, the British athletes enjoyed mixed fortunes. A below par Steve Cram failed to qualify for the 800m final and missed out on a medal in the 1500m. Peter Elliott, bravely running through a torn groin muscle, took the silver in the 1500m as did Colin Jackson (110m hurdles) and the men's 4x100m relay team. Fatima Whitbread took silver in the javelin, Liz McColgan matched this in the 10,000m and Yvonne Murray came third in the 3000m. Seven Olympic medals but no gold.

What about the athletes?

The following year, 1989, was the year when the athletes really did save the sport in Britain.

The European Cup was held in Gateshead, the stamping ground of Brendan Foster, Steve Cram and others. Held over two days, the Cup is the European championship of nations and the winning team can rightly claim to be Europe's top athletic country. Great Britain had never won this competition.

The men's team got off to a good start when Kriss Akabusi surpassed himself to win the opening track event, the 400m hurdles, and, at the end of the first day of competition, the team was in first place, leading the Soviet Union, favourites for the title, by 11 points. Could they hold on?

The team spirit continued through the second day but, by the start of the final event, the Soviet Union had narrowed the gap to a single point. All would depend on the last event, the 4x400m relay, but Great Britain had a good record internationally in this and finished triumphantly in first place.

The capacity crowd was delirious but team manager Les Jones suddenly realised that there was no appointed team captain to collect the trophy. There could be only one choice and Linford Christie was appointed captain on the spot.

As has been described elsewhere, this unexpected result was the crucial factor in convincing ITV to renew its long term contract to broadcast British athletics.

The icing on the cake was that the women's team finished in third place, equalling their best ever performance in the competition.

By winning in Gateshead, the British men qualified to take part in the World Cup in Barcelona at the end of the season.

The World Cup, organised by the IAAF, was a hybrid competition between eight teams; representing continents, the best European national teams and the USA. Against the best in the world, the British team finished third, behind winners USA and the continental European team. Somewhat hidden amongst the world class performances, was a break through by a British athlete who was to become a household name – triple jumper Jonathan Edwards won his first significant international competition.

What about the athletes?

As the decade of the eighties ended and that of the nineties began, a new group of star athletes was putting British athletics on the map. Linford Christie and Colin Jackson already had Olympic medals and Jonathan Edwards, Steve Backley and Roger Black had shown what they could do. Not to be outdone by the men, Liz McColgan and Yvonne Murray were already world class and Sally Gunnell was challenging for stardom.

In 1990, the European Championships were held in Split, in what is now Croatia. Britain has traditionally done well at European Championships and this was to prove no exception.

Steve Backley (already the world record holder) and Linford Christie got the team off to a good start with wins in the javelin and 100m respectively. The medals piled up and, in all, Britain won 9 gold medals, 5 silver and 4 bronze. This outstanding medal haul, however, concealed Britain's Achilles heels; all the medals except one (Backley's) were won in track events and, despite the team's third place in the previous year's European Cup, there was only one individual women's medal, that of Yvonne Murray in the 3000m.

1991 was another busy year for the athletes but was also a big year for the administrators as, at long last, the BAF was voted into being and took over the management of the sport on 1st October of that year.

The reigning European men's team champions travelled to Frankfurt for the European Cup and narrowly failed to retain its title, losing to the victorious Soviet Union by a mere 2.5 points, the women again coming third.

After the euphoria of the previous European Championships, the 1991 world championships in Tokyo would be a stern test for the new stars of the British team. Although winning a creditable 8 medals in all, there was only one individual gold, from Liz McColgan-Lynch in the 10,000m, but the final event of the entire championships was Britain's to savour when Kriss Akabusi won the dramatic drive to the line and took gold in the 4x400m relay, the thickness of his vest ahead of the USA.

In late 1991, a few months after its formation, the BAF received a proposal for an international match against South Africa, to take place in South Africa the following year. South Africa had long been the pariah of international sport because of its apartheid policies and British athletics had already received a bruising over the Zola Budd affair.

What about the athletes?

By 1991, however, South African sport was starting to get its act together, had come close to readmission to the IAAF in late 1991 and had high hopes of taking part in the Olympic Games in Barcelona in 1992 as, in fact, it did. It may have been something of a coup, therefore, for Great Britain to be the first country to welcome South Africa back from the sporting wilderness by sending a team to compete against them. Moreover, a high percentage of the British team was black.

However, once news of the possible fixture crept out, there was an immediate backlash from some of Britain's leading black athletes who declared that they would refuse to compete in South Africa. Star British athletes including Linford Christie, Tony Jarrett, John Regis and Derek Redmond led a potential boycott.

The timing was unfortunate as strong moves were taking place to reintroduce South Africa to the world community of sport but the BAF had misjudged the reactions of the athletes and the match never took place.

After the comparative disappointment of Seoul four years earlier, the Barcelona Olympic Games of 1992 brought triumph and disappointment alike for Great Britain. Two gold medals from Linford Christie (100m) and Sally Gunnell (400m hurdles) were the highlights followed by bronze medals from Kriss Akabusi (400m hurdles), Steve Backley (javelin) and both men's and women's 4x400m teams. The disappointment was Colin Jackson's failure to get amongst the medals despite being the favourite for the gold.

A few weeks after the Olympic Games, the World Junior Championships took place in Seoul, South Korea. One of Britain's strongest junior teams included future Olympic medallists Darren Campbell, Iwan Thomas, Jamie Baulch, Steve Smith and Katherine Merry as well as a quiet young lady who was to become one of Britain's and world athletics' greatest stars – Paula Radcliffe.

The treadmill never stopped and 1993 brought another world championships, this time in Stuttgart, Germany and the first of the change from a four yearly to a biennial championship.

Colin Jackson came back from his Olympic disappointment with a roar, taking the gold medal in the 110m hurdles and setting a new world record in the process. Sally Gunnell did the same in the 400m hurdles, winning in a new world record time, and Linford Christie showed that his Olympic Gold was no fluke by winning the world title. Silver medals came

What about the athletes?

from Tony Jarrett (110m hurdles) and John Regis (200m) and bronze from Steve Smith (high jump), Jonathan Edwards (triple jump), Mick Hill (pushing Steve Backley into 4th place in the javelin) and the women's 4x400m relay team.

1994 brought another European Championship, this time in Helsinki, a Mecca of athletics where javelin throwing is a national sport.

Britain was, as usual, expected to do well and did not disappoint. Six gold medals came from Linford Christie (100m), Du'aine Ladejo (400m), Colin Jackson (110m hurdles), Steve Backley (javelin), Sally Gunnell (400m hurdles) and the men's 4x400m team. Silver medals were won by Roger Black (400m), Rob Denmark (5000m), Kelly Holmes (1500m) and Yvonne Murray (3000m) while Tony Jarrett (110m hurdles), Steve Smith (high jump) and Phyllis Smith (400m) took bronze.

Once again, Great Britain was shown to be one of the leading athletic nations in Europe.

The 1995 World championships in Gothenburg, Sweden, will forever be remembered as Jonathan Edwards' championships. Not only did he take the gold medal in the triple jump but he broke the world record twice during the competition, concluding with a breathtaking 18.29m which still remains unbroken. A sign of things to come had been seen earlier in the season during the European Cup in Lille where he jumped a phenomenal but wind assisted 18.43m.

Elsewhere, Britain had a less successful championship. With Christie, Jackson and Gunnell retired or retiring, only 4 other medals were won. Tony Jarrett and Steve Backley each took a silver medal and Kelly Holmes took silver in the 1500m and bronze in the 800m.

1995 was notable for a chilling in relationships between the BAF and the leading athletes and I have already described the row with Colin Jackson over the AAA championships and the later boycott of an event by Christie, Jackson and others.

This was potentially very damaging to both the BAF and the athletes but, fortunately, through the enlightened attitude of senior athletes Roger Black and Geoff Parsons and a wish by BAF chairman Peter Radford to mend the rift, a solution was eventually found in the shape of a British Athletes' Association. The deal negotiated by Radford, Black and Parsons was that the management of the sport would be reorganised and

What about the athletes?

the athletes, through their association, given a direct say and stake in the televised events.

The British Athletes Association would effectively be a modern version of the former International Athletes Club that had folded in 1993 after it lost its TV contract and ran out of money. The Association was eventually launched in September 1996 with an initial board of directors that, significantly, included both Christie and Jackson.

Atlanta, USA, was the venue for the 1996 Olympic Games with Britain under the spotlight after its two gold medals in Barcelona four years before. It was not to be a repeat performance and, although British athletes won more medals, there was no gold.

Jonathan Edwards could not quite live up to his pre-Olympic billing as favourite and returned home with a silver medal, along with Steve Backley, Roger Black and the men's 4x400m relay team. Denise Lewis took the heptathlon bronze and Steve Smith won bronze in the high jump.

1997 dawned and with it another world championships, this time in Athens, the home of the first Olympics of the modern era in 1886. Many had expected Athens to be chosen to stage the centenary edition of the Olympic Games in 1996 but the city had missed out to Atlanta and would have wait another eight years before hosting the 2004 Games.

With bankruptcy looming for the cash strapped BAF, the money was nevertheless found to send a team to Athens. It was a relatively disappointing championship as Britain returned home without a gold medal, the yardstick of real success.

Five silver medals were won by Colin Jackson (110m hurdles), Jonathan Edwards (triple jump), Steve Backley (javelin), Denise Lewis (heptathlon) and the men's 4x400m and 4x100m relay teams. Some years later, the 4x400m silver medal was elevated to gold when the winning USA team was disqualified following a doping confession by Antonio Pettigrew.

The gloom over the results from Athens was matched by that within the BAF which filed for administration a few weeks later.

During this long period from the early eighties to the late nineties, British athletes had maintained Britain's excellent international reputation with strings of world class performances and this is described in detail in Tony Ward's fascinating book "*The Golden Decade*". Sadly, the

What about the athletes?

administrators of the sport were not able to match the achievements of the athletes.

Tony Ward had been the long serving Press Officer of the AAA/BAAB/BAF and had striven to present British Athletics in the best possible light. This often seemed to be an impossible task, trying to balance the outstanding performances of athletes with sometimes simultaneous administrative controversies.

An ever present worry was the shadow of doping cases involving British athletes and these cropped up all too often. Perversely, athletics as a sport was paying a heavy price for its leadership in the campaign against doping cheats and Britain was a leader within athletics. A further complication was that sportsmen of all kinds were referred to in the media as athletes and a quite erroneous link with the sport of athletics was often made. Tony Ward was alert to this inequity but, try as he might, the press were rarely interested to keep the record straight.

EPILOGUE

I decided to write this account some 13 years after I had given up the Honorary Treasurership of the BAF, having subsequently spent 12 years as an elected member of the Council of the European Athletic Association.

Within the EAA I quickly found myself doing much the same work (TV and sponsor negotiations and event organisation) as in the AAA-BAAB/BAF and have wondered why I found this period so enjoyable and fulfilling whereas my time in Britain was so arduous and, at times, unpleasant. There are a few key reasons.

Firstly, the EAA is a stable and respected organisation within the sport in Europe and the rest of the world. Its primary role is to organise championship events which themselves have great credibility; the European Championships were for long the most important athletic event apart from the Olympic Games and, even now, are second only to the World Athletic Championships. The Officers and Council members are elected for four year periods which give them the stability and confidence to make sometimes difficult decisions without constantly looking over their shoulders to next year's elections. As a result of these stabilising factors, the atmosphere and relationships between the individuals is friendly and supportive. This is not to say that mistakes or criticisms are never made but one does not find the animosity which was the hallmark of athletics in Britain.

In contrast, athletics in Britain has rarely been comfortable in its own skin and there has hardly been a time when there was not one ginger or lobby group or another. British athletics has always needed to be dragged kicking and screaming from the past into the future, usually with a three party war between those who want to maintain the status quo at all costs, those who promote a plan for what they see as progress and a third group that agrees basically with the aims of the second group but knows better. A system that demanded all senior positions to be elected annually meant that there was little stability or real continuity, with an annual opportunity for the malcontents to wreak their damage.

In addition, the programme of televised events that provided the financial bedrock of the sport for so long was itself controversial as many in the sport (at all levels) considered the events and the relationship with television to be artificial and unhealthy for the "real" sport. Thus there was, and to some extent remains, a lack of the credibility that the EAA's championships programme enjoys.

The traumas of the creation and eventual demise of the BAF were necessary but poorly managed steps towards the modernisation of athletics in Britain and some good has come from it. At least there are no longer separate organisations for men and women, cross country and road and it is now almost unbelievable that this should ever have been so. It is taken for granted that championships for men and women are held together; why should it have been such a battle to achieve this? The bankruptcy of the BAF was certainly a major shock to the sport but enabled it to implement a far more radical overhaul of its structures than would otherwise have been possible.

The reasons for BAF's failure were essentially that the sport was unstable and unwilling to embrace the changes needed. The clubs had forced the AAA to accept the need to change but the traditionalists never really wanted to give up what they thought was their heritage.

The English, in particular, fought a rearguard action throughout and rarely missed an opportunity to undermine the fragile stability of the BAF. They refused to properly fund the BAF at the outset and built up their own funds at BAF's expense, denying help when the BAF was on the brink of bankruptcy and needed it most.

The Celtic nations had gone along with the reforms but with no great enthusiasm and became, not exactly silent, but certainly relatively docile partners within BAF. It was usual that the vast majority of the talking at meetings came from the representatives of the English regions and it was not unknown for some from, say, Scotland or Wales to spend a whole weekend in meetings of the BAF Council and say nothing throughout.

I have often wondered why there was also such a level of, frequently personal, animosity at so many meetings and between those representing the different elements of the sport. This had reached a pitch within the AAA and the expectation that relationships would settle down once the BAF was formed was not realised. Most of the members of the Council, Management Board, Regional Associations, etc. were perfectly decent people who had spent their lives devoting endless hours to the sport that they loved but, for reasons that have mystified me, often

Epilogue

seemed to leave these qualities outside whilst inside the corridors of power.

The model adopted by BAF's successor, UK Athletics, is totally different; indeed it is close to being unique in Europe. Of the principal positions, only the President and Vice President are elected by the clubs of the UK and this has resulted in a more professional and self contained organisation, free from the political strife of its predecessors. As a result of groundwork started in the last days of BAF and carried on by David Moorcroft, UK Athletics wields a considerable budget, enjoys substantial revenues from television (the BBC!) and sponsors and promotes largely the same series of commercial events as those developed by the IAC and Andy Norman.

But the early transition to UKA was not seamless. David Moorcroft had been persuaded to create a new governing body but inherited a system that was out of date. He commissioned an independent review by Sir Andrew Foster that recommended, amongst other things, the wholesale restructuring of the sport in England. An entirely new entity, England Athletics, was established to administer the sport through nine geographical regions that matched those of the English Sports Council. The old AAA of England (which reverted to its historic name Amateur Athletic Association), along with its three regional associations, were to be given minor roles and allowed to wither on the vine. The arrangements in Scotland, Wales and Northern Ireland, however, would continue substantially unchanged.

Thus the once powerful AAA has, at the time of writing, been reduced to a minor player in the sport, with little or no income and simply expending its reserves year after year to maintain a presence.

But UKA itself is still criticised by the sport – for being undemocratic and unaccountable.

It is hard to blame UKA for not wishing to recreate the "democracy" under which its predecessors laboured but it has less defence against any charges of unaccountability as there is every reason why UKA, as the governing federation of athletics in the UK, should explain and justify its existence and activities. Its duties to lead the sport and to account for its performance could easily be met by more effective communication. As ever, the clubs feel isolated and neglected as UKA and its regional organisations appear bureaucratic and to command large budgets which never seem to reach them, the poor foot soldiers.

Epilogue

It has also been responsible for creating what can only be regarded as an administrative mess in England where there exist both the AAA, overseeing three geographical regions (North, South, Midlands) with little to do, and England Athletics, overseeing nine geographical regions and wielding a substantial budget that is dependent on the continued flow of Sports Council and Lottery grants. It says much for the personnel involved that relative harmony prevails but the mismatch leaves the potential for tension in the future.

Paradoxically, with more resources than the old organisations ever had (in its financial year to March 2010, UKA turned over £25 million, had over 100 full and part time employees and spent £8.5m on funding athletes), the performances of British athletes on the international stage initially disappointed compared with those of the previous decades when there was a direct link between athletes' performances in competition and their income.

After an excellent Olympic Games in Sydney in 2000 which yielded six individual medals including golds from Jonathan Edwards and Denise Lewis, the medal count dwindled. The world championships in 2001 produced only 1 gold (Edwards) and 1 bronze; in 2003 only 1 silver and two bronze (no gold); and in 2005 1 gold (Paula Radcliffe) and 2 bronze. There was an improvement at the Olympic Games in 2004 when Kelly Holmes took 2 gold medals alongside Kelly Sotherton's bronze in the Heptathlon and a further gold from the men's 4x100m relay but the world championships in Osaka in 2007 did mark the start of what appears to be an improvement, with 5 medals but only one gold (Christine Orohuogu in the 400m). The 2008 Olympic Games were more successful than expected and the world championships in Berlin in 2009 even more so, with 6 medals including 2 gold.

The 2010 European Championships in Barcelona produced a record haul of 19 medals, including 6 gold, one more than the 18 medals won in Split in 1990. Great Britain was second to Russia in the overall national rankings and British athletics was once again riding high. A sterner test, however, would lie ahead with the 2011 IAAF World Championships in Daegu, South Korea.

Much hope is being pinned on the Olympic and Paralympic Games in London in 2012 to provide the inspiration for and the legacy of a new generation of successful British athletes.

Epilogue

It will also be crucial that UK athletics retains the services of the ageing armies of voluntary officials and coaches on whom the majority of the sport depends. Furthermore the renewal of lucrative television and sponsorship agreements in a post Olympic and potentially still critical economic environment will determine whether UK Athletics and its high spending satellite organisations can continue to deliver the levels of employment and services that have been built up.

Let's hope it all succeeds.

WHERE ARE THEY NOW?

David Bedford

After losing his position as Honorary Secretary of the BAF in 1994, David Bedford has gone on to make a successful career as Race Director of the London Marathon.

John Bromley

After resigning as head of sport at ITV in 1993, John Bromley became a television consultant and chairman of the independent Television Sport and Leisure (TSL). Bromley died in 2002.

Frank Dick

After resigning from the BAF, Frank Dick established a career as a consultant and motivational speaker. He is currently President of the European Coaches Association and Chairman of Scottish Athletics.

Bill Evans

After retiring as chairman of the BAF in 1993, Bill Evans substantially withdrew from athletics and died two years later, in 1995

Mike Farrell

Mike Farrell retired as General Secretary of the BAF following the appointment of Malcolm Jones as Chief Executive and became a sales consultant for a leading sports equipment manufacturer. Now retired, he has moved to the West Country.

Where are they now?

Marea Hartman

Following the reorganisation of athletics in 1991, Marea Hartman became President of the AAA of England. She died in 1994, the same year that she was made a Dame of the British Empire.

Derek Johnson

Derek Johnson became the Honorary Secretary of the AAA of England in 1991 but relinquished his position two years later. To the surprise of many, he re-married but died in 2004.

John Lister

After serving three terms on the Council of the European Athletic Association, John Lister has continued to work for his club in Cardiff. He was awarded the MBE in 2010 for services to athletics.

Arthur McAllister

Arthur McAllister substantially withdrew from athletics after handing over the Presidency of the BAF to Mary Peters in 1994. He was awarded an OBE in 1994 and died in 2006.

Where are they now?

David Moorcroft

David Moorcroft inherited a sport in chaos following the demise of the BAF and remained Chief Executive of UK Athletics until 2006. He is currently working as a consultant.

Andy Norman

Following his sacking from the BAF, Andy Norman continued to play an active part in international athletics as an athletes' agent and adviser to numerous event organisers in Europe. He died suddenly in 2007, returning from the World Athletic Final in Stuttgart.

Alan Pascoe

Alan Pascoe's company played a pivotal role in the revival of the commercial events of athletics during and after the transition to UK Athletics through his company Fast Track Events, where he is chairman and which he has built up to be a significant consultancy to several major sports.

Peter Radford

Following his resignation from the BAF in 1997, Peter Radford returned to university life, becoming Professor of Sports Science at Brunel University until he retired to live in the Cotswolds and pursue his interests in writing and the history of sport.

Where are they now?

Richard Russell

After leaving ITV, Richard Russell became a television consultant and is currently an executive with Fast Track Events where he has led the modernisation of in-stadium event presentation of athletics.

Roger Simons

Upon the formation of UK Athletics, Roger Simons joined its board of directors with a special interest in competition planning. He was elected to the supervisory Members' Council in 2009.

Ian Stewart

Having taken over responsibility for the events department following Andy Norman's sudden departure, Ian Stewart has continued in this role ever since. He was given responsibility for overseeing the development of Britain's middle distance talent in 2009.

Tony Ward

Since parting company with the BAF in early 1997 Tony Ward continued to be a writer and shrewd observer of the athletics scene. He moved to the Lake District with his wife Gwenda. He died in 2010.

PAST OFFICERS

AAA – Presidents:

Victor A G C Villiers, Earl of Jersey	1880-1890
Richard E Webster, Viscount Alverstone	1891-1915
Sir Montague Shearman	1916-1930
Baron Desborough of Taplow	1930-1936
Marquess of Exeter	1936-1976
Harold M Abrahams	1976-1978
Squire Yarrow	1978-1982
Ronald Goodman	1982-1986
Arthur G McAllister	1986-1991

BAF – Presidents:

Arthur G McAllister	1991-1994
Mary Peters	1994-1997

AAA – Honorary Secretaries:

Sir Montague Shearman	1880-1883
Charles Herbert	1883-1906
Percy L Fisher	1906-1915
Sir Harry Barclay	1915-1931
Douglas G A Lowe	1931-1938
Ernest J H Holt	1938-1947
Ernest H L Clynes	1947-1965
Barry Willis	1965-1982
Michael A Farrell (General Secretary – professional)	1982-1991

BAF – Honorary Secretaries:

David Bedford	1991-1994
Matt Frazer	1994-1997

Past officers

AAA – Honorary Treasurers:

Clement N Jackson	1880-1910
William M Barnard	1910-1932
Ernest J H Holt	1932-1938
Claude W F Pearce	1938-1947
Walter C Jewell	1947-1957
Arthur D Thwaites	1957-1960
Philip S Gale	1960-1966
George B Cooper	1966-1967
Frank J B Read	1967-1970
F John Martell	1970-1974
Raymond L Stroud	1974-1980
F John Martell	1980-1985
David Cropper	1985-1986
John T Lister	1986-1991

BAF – Honorary Treasurers:

John T Lister	1991-1996
Martin J R Evanson	1996-1997
Keith W Atkins	1997

AAA – Chairman of the General Committee:

B R Wise		1880-1882
W Waddell		1882
Sir Montague Shearman		1883-1909
G V A Schofield	)	
G B Holmes	)	
A Fattorini	)	
T M Abraham	)	
H A Butler	)	
G T Pratt	)	
P Fisher	)	1909-1939
W W Alexander	)	
A Machin	)	
W T Rainbow	)	
H F Pash	)	
D Lyons	)	
J W Turner	)	
H M Abrahams	)	
J W Turner		1940

Past officers

H F Pash	1941
E Tomlinson	1942
J W Turner	1942
H F Pash	1943
E Tomlinson	1944
T H Blair	1945
J H Greenaway	1946
Arthur Turk	1946-1950
J Willie Turner	1950-1965
Sidney Best	1966-1967
Eric Kennell	1967-1969
Ronald Goodman	1970-1975
Leslie Golding	1976-1980
Arthur G McAllister	1981-1986
William J Ferguson	1987-1988
William A L Evans	1989-1991

BAF – Chairman of the Council:

William A L Evans	1991-1993
Peter F Radford	1993
Kenneth W Rickhuss	1993-1997